On Epistemology

On Epistemology

Linda Zagzebski
University of Oklahoma

WADSWORTH
CENGAGE Learning™

Australia • Brazil • Japan • Korea • Mexico • Singapore • Spain • United Kingdom • United States

On Epistemology
Linda Zagzebski

Discipline Editor: Clark Baxter

Assistant Editor: Sarah Perkins

Marketing Manager: Christina Shea

Marketing Assistant: Mary Anne Payumo

Marketing Communications Manager: Darlene Amidon-Brent

Project Manager, Editorial Production: Samen Iqbal

Creative Director: Rob Hugel

Art Director: Cate Barr

Print Buyer: Elizabeth Donaghey

Production Service: Tintu Thomas, Integra

Copy Editor: Linda Ireland

Compositor: Integra

For product information and technology assistance, contact us at **Cengage Learning Customer & Sales Support, 1-800-354-9706**

For permission to use material from this text or product, submit all requests online at **www.cengage.com/permissions**
Further permissions questions can be emailed to **permissionrequest@cengage.com**

Library of Congress Control Number: 2008929205

ISBN-13: 978-0-534-25234-2

ISBN-10: 0-534-25234-6

Wadsworth
20 Davis Drive
Belmont, CA 94002
USA

Cengage Learning is a leading provider of customized learning solutions with office locations around the globe, including Singapore, the United Kingdom, Australia, Mexico, Brazil, and Japan. Locate your local office at **www.cengage.com/global**

Cengage Learning products are represented in Canada by Nelson Education, Ltd.

To learn more about Wadsworth, visit
www.cengage.com/wadsworth

Purchase any of our products at your local college store or at our preferred online store **www.CengageBrain.com**

Printed in the United States of America
2 3 4 5 6 7 11 10 09

Brief Contents

Contents

CONTENTS

Acknowledgments

I am very grateful to my research assistants, Eric Yang and Timothy Miller, for their splendid work on this book. I thank Ray Elugardo for his valuable comments on Chapter Three, Robert Roberts and Jay Wood for their comments on Chapter Four, and Stephen Grimm for a very interesting discussion on understanding after he read a draft of Chapter Six. John Greco provided detailed and very helpful comments on Chapters Four and Five, and Trent Dougherty and the students in Wayne Riggs's epistemology seminar also sent me comments on those chapters, helping me to improve a number of points on intellectual virtues and knowledge. Finally, I want to thank Scott Aikin, who read and commented on the entire manuscript, and whose suggestions have been incorporated throughout the book.

1

Epistemic Value and What We Care About

I. INTRODUCTION

Epistemology is the philosophical study of knowing and other desirable ways of believing and attempting to find the truth. It is a central field of philosophy because it links the two most important objects of philosophical inquiry: ourselves and the world. Of course, knowing is not the only way in which we are linked with the world, but it is a crucial one. Plato had the fascinating idea that knowledge has interesting similarities with love because love and knowledge are the two ways in which we are drawn out of ourselves, first to a world that reflects the eternal Forms, and then, with luck and the proper discipline, to the world of Forms themselves.[1] Love is not usually discussed in a book of epistemology, but it is helpful to notice that knowledge is only one of our links to the outside. Philosophers sometimes worry that if there is no knowledge, we are forced into **solipsism**, the view that we are locked inside our own minds. That worry is based on the assumption that of all threads that tie us to the world, knowledge is the most basic, so if you break the thread of knowledge, you break your connection to the world. On this picture, knowledge is a lifeline that keeps us attached to the world and

---

[1] See Socrates' speech in the *Symposium*, esp. 210a–212c.

prevents us from floating away in a world of our own imagination. Of course, that might not be true, but it is a captivating idea.

Most of the central questions of epistemology, then, pertain to knowledge: What is knowledge? Is knowledge possible? How do we get it? These three questions are intertwined and it is not obvious which question comes first. For example, you might think we cannot work on the issue of whether knowledge is possible before figuring out what knowledge is, but some philosophers have been accused of imposing conditions on knowledge that are unreasonably stringent, thereby leading to the conclusion that knowledge is unattainable. But if knowledge on some account turns out to be unattainable, you might conclude that there is something wrong with the account.

Compare the issue in ethics of what a good life is. If it turned out that on some theory of a good life nobody has a good life, you might think that there is something wrong with the view. That is because you might take it as obvious that some people lead a good life. Similarly, many philosophers take it as obvious that some people have knowledge; in fact, we probably all do. If so, no account of knowledge is acceptable unless it is compatible with the position that knowledge is attainable. But notice that if you think that, you are treating the question "Is knowledge possible?" as settled prior to raising the question "What is knowledge?" Of course, you might be mistaken, but your position deserves a hearing. In any case, it is not obvious which of the two questions comes first.

What about the question of how we get knowledge? That question also is not clearly one we should wait to address until after we answer the question "What is knowledge?" It is only in the modern period that philosophers asked what knowledge is before addressing metaphysical questions, including the question of what human beings are like and the capacities we have. The ways in which we perceive and cognize the world are part of human nature. If you imitate the ancient and medieval philosophers and begin with metaphysics before doing epistemology, you would normally expect to treat knowledge as something that comes out of a study of human nature. What we call "knowledge" is the product of cognitive interaction with the world when all goes as it should. According to that approach, it makes more sense to investigate how the world is put together and our place in it before asking what knowledge is. The answer to the question "How do we get knowl-edge?" therefore comes before the answer to the question "What is knowledge?," so again, it is not obvious which question comes first. This point is important because epistemology can look very different when you start with one of these questions rather than another.

Perhaps the central feature of knowledge, one that virtually everyone accepts, now and in the past, is that it is a state that puts us in *cognitive contact with reality*. Almost everybody also agrees that knowledge is a *good state*. It is unlikely that epistemology would be a major branch of philosophy were it not for the fact that we think it is the study of states we desire to have. In Plato's *Protagoras*, Socrates mentions and eventually defends the view that the only real kind of faring ill is the loss of knowledge (345b). To the modern mind that may sound excessively dramatic, but even so, most of us would be upset if we thought we could not get knowledge. Whether or not we think knowledge is our tether to the world outside us, we assume it is a good thing to have it and a bad thing to lack it, at least in general.

Given these assumptions, a rough philosophical consensus has developed on the following features of knowledge:

(1) Knowing is a relation between a conscious subject and an object, where the object (but possibly not the immediate object) is some portion of reality.

(2) The relation is cognitive. That is to say, the subject thinks, not just senses or feels the object. More specifically,

(3) Knowing includes believing.

In the fifth century St. Augustine defined believing as thinking with assent, a definition that would be widely accepted today.[2] Some people use the terms "believe" and "know" in a way that makes them mutually exclusive, but as long as believing is just thinking with assent, there is a consensus that knowing is a form of believing.

Thinking is a state that has an object. When we think with assent, there is something to which we assent. So when we know, there is an object of thought to which we assent. It is customary to call this object a proposition. So another component of the philosophical consensus about knowledge is:

(4) The object of knowledge is a proposition.

The nature of propositions is a metaphysical issue that is generally not treated in epistemology. This might seem puzzling, but it is understandable if you consider that the proposition is at the object

---

[2] *A Treatise on the Predestination of the Saints*, bk. I, ch. 5. Reprinted in Augustine and Collinge (1992).

end of the knowing relation, whereas epistemology focuses mostly on the subject end of the relation and the knowing relation itself. We will not investigate the debate about what a proposition is in this book, but will try to be neutral on the issue.

Philosophers almost always agree that a proposition has a syntactical form. Its structure is like the structure of a sentence, but a proposition is not the same as a sentence. A proposition is the content of a sentence, the information you get from a sentence. So different sentences can express the same proposition, such as the English sentence "It is raining" and the French sentence "Il pleut," and two different English sentences can express the same proposition, such as "The exam is tomorrow," asserted on Tuesday, and "The exam was yesterday," asserted on Thursday. Further, a single sentence such as "The exam is tomorrow" can express one proposition when asserted on Tuesday and a different proposition when asserted on Thursday. So what you know when you know that the exam is tomorrow is not a sentence, but what the sentence conveys, its content.

Using sentences to refer to the objects of knowledge makes the epistemologist's job of discussing potential instances of knowledge easier. We can discuss whether Jane knows that snow is white, whether Jim knows that his next-door neighbor is a spy, whether anybody knows that there is a God or that the theory of evolution is true, and so on. In each case the expression following "knows that" has a sentential form, and by knowing a language, we all have a ready-made list of potential objects of knowledge that we can discuss with other speakers of our language.

Not every proposition can be an object of knowledge, however. Knowledge is limited to the domain of true propositions, so another feature of knowledge that epistemologists agree about is this:

(5) The object of knowledge is a true proposition.

You cannot know a proposition that isn't true. Granted, you might firmly believe a false proposition. It might seem to *you* that you know it, but you don't. All knowing is believing, but not all believing is knowing. Some believing is not knowing because it is directed at the wrong thing—a false proposition. I might believe that the small tree with the dark-colored leaves growing in my back yard is a plum tree, and I might even be dead sure that it is a plum, but if it is not a plum, I cannot know that it is. The fact that the objects of knowledge are limited to what is true is one of the ways we must humbly submit to the world. With few exceptions, we do not get to decide the way the world is, and if we want knowledge, we don't get to decide which of our beliefs count as knowledge.

Even though most philosophers agree that knowledge is directed at true propositions, they almost always also agree that this is not exactly true, since there is nonpropositional knowledge. One can have nonpropositional knowledge of other persons, of oneself and one's own mental states, and other objects in one's environment which one knows by direct experience rather than through testimony or inference from other things one knows. But most epistemologists choose to ignore nonpropositional knowledge for at least two reasons: (1) It is very difficult to analyze it and it is hard to say anything about it that adds to our understanding of it, and (2) It is so different from propositional knowledge that it needs a separate treatment. In most of this book I will follow the convention of concentrating on propositional knowledge, but it is helpful to keep in mind that not all knowledge is propositional.

A feature of the consensus about knowledge that will play an important role in this book is this:

(6) Knowing is a good state.

It is good at least in the sense of desirable, and it is even more desirable than mere true belief. Aristotle thought that wanting knowledge is an intrinsic part of human nature, and he begins his *Metaphysics* with the declaration, "All men by nature desire to know." Ordinary people may not ask themselves "What is knowledge?," but they do try to find out the answers to their questions, and they also try to find out whether the answers they accept are things they then know. So knowledge is good and it is good enough that it is worth some effort to get it and some effort to figure out how to get it.

If we put together these relatively uncontroversial features of knowledge, we get the following: *To know is to believe a true proposition in a good way.* Much of Chapter Five will be devoted to different answers to the question, "What makes knowing good?" This also is a question that is not obviously subsequent to the question "What is knowledge?" I think that any acceptable answer to the question "What is knowledge?" must be compatible with a reasonable answer to the question "What makes knowledge good?," but the latter question is surprisingly hard to answer because different epistemic values have dominated philosophy at different times in history. The two most general values are **understanding** and **certainty**. Each of them has dominated epistemology for long periods, but rarely, if ever, at the same time. I suspect that that has an interesting consequence for the attempt to discuss knowledge across different historical periods. In Hellenistic philosophy (ancient Greek philosophy after Aristotle) and most modern philosophy after Descartes, certainty was given more attention than understanding, while in Plato and Aristotle, in the long medieval period, and even in some of the major modern philosophers such as Spinoza, it was the reverse. Usually whichever one of the two values dominated was the one connected with the concept of knowledge, so Plato comes very close to identifying knowledge with understanding, while Descartes comes very close to identifying knowledge with certainty.

Historians have attributed this difference in focus to differences in the way skepticism was handled. I said earlier that one of the central questions of epistemology is whether knowledge is possible. Some philosophers have answered no, and others have said that there is no adequate response to those who say no even if they do not give a negative answer themselves. Skeptical periods are those in which this position is widespread. We have been living in a skeptical period for almost four hundred years, although many philosophers are trying to put skepticism behind us. Skeptical periods have generally been accompanied by the concern for certainty and the process of justifying belief, since **justification** is what is needed to defend the right to be sure. In contrast, the nonskeptical periods have been mostly concerned with understanding, and the questions accompanying it show little concern for justification but, instead, an interest in the process of **explanation**, since the ability to explain displays one's understanding.

It seems to me that this difference between the focus on certainty and the focus on understanding affects the way knowledge is defined. In the eras in which certainty was the dominant value and skepticism was treated in full seriousness, knowledge was often defined, roughly, as believing a true proposition in a justified way. So knowledge is **justified true belief**. This definition was masterfully defended by Roderick Chisholm (1964), a leader of later twentieth-century epistemology, and this account of knowledge dominated epistemology for decades. Because it was part of the consensus until recently, it still shapes the way many epistemologists approach knowledge.

In contrast, in eras in which understanding was the dominant value and skepticism was not perceived as threatening, knowledge was defined very differently. In Plato's *Theaetetus* (201d) Socrates considers (and eventually rejects) the definition of knowledge (*epistêmê*) as true belief plus a *logos* (an account or explanation). A *logos* is nothing like a justification. In fact, the ability to give a *logos* is more like a capacity that a person has because of her mastery of a skill (*technê*). A person who can give a *logos* knows how to do something well, and this makes her a trustworthy person to consult in matters pertaining to the skill in question. It is doubtful that Plato thought of the object of knowledge as a discrete proposition, nor did he think that the relation between knower and the object known is belief. So Plato might well have rejected all three of the components of the twentieth-century justified-true-belief account of knowledge.

Notice that if we approach knowledge from the point of view of the value of understanding, we would have to give up the third and fourth elements of the consensus about knowledge mentioned earlier. Knowledge might still be a cognitive state that puts the subject in relation to reality outside her mind, and it would still be a good state, but it would not be a state of assenting to a discrete proposition. Knowledge might involve mental representations, but rather than to know exclusively through objects with the structure of sentences, one could know through many other kinds of structures, including maps, graphs, diagrams, and models. Some forms of understanding might not even involve representations. What happens when we understand a work of art or music, the psychological structure of a character in a novel, or a theory in physics? Do we have a kind of knowledge? If so, would it be accurate to say that what we know is reducible to a list of propositions? I find that dubious, and I suspect that contemporary epistemology has suffered by ignoring the value of understanding. I also suspect that understanding is connected with nonpropositional knowledge, which, as I mentioned earlier, is usually left aside in contemporary treatments of knowledge.

So while I am identifying the features of knowledge that epistemologists generally accept, I also think it is significant to notice that some features of this consensus are quite different from what philosophers have thought at other periods of history. It would be helpful to keep this in mind as we go through this book because it can give us a sense of proportion about what we are doing, and perhaps give us ideas when we encounter problems that appear insurmountable.

An interesting feature of epistemology today is that the consensus is starting to break down. About a quarter century ago Richard Rorty (1979) became known for proclaiming that epistemology is dead.

What Rorty and the other death-of-epistemology theorists (e.g., Michael Williams, 1991) claimed is that epistemology is a branch of philosophy that is devoted to answering skepticism, but if skepticism is not threatening, then epistemology loses its point. As we will see in Chapters Two and Three, the history of modern epistemology makes a great deal of sense if read as the history of responses to skepticism, but it does not follow that without skepticism there is nothing for epistemologists to do. In my opinion, one of the things philosophers need to do is to recover the value of understanding. For other things we need to do, let us go back to the central questions of epistemology.

I began with three important questions: What is knowledge? Is knowledge attainable? How do we get knowledge? I also mentioned that since we think of knowledge as a good way to believe, another important question to ask is why we want knowledge. What is good about it? Certainty and understanding are values that have been associated with knowledge at different periods of history, so this leads to two other sets of questions: (1) What is certainty, is it attainable, and how do we get it? (2) What is understanding, is it attainable, and how do we get it? There are also questions in epistemology that are not about knowledge, although they might be confused with questions about knowledge. Epistemologists investigate good and bad ways to form and revise our beliefs. Knowing is one good way to have a belief, but there are others. Some beliefs are reasonable and others unreasonable. Some beliefs are intellectually virtuous and others vicious. We can form and keep beliefs carefully or carelessly, open-mindedly or close-mindedly, fairly or unfairly, with intelligent sensitivity to the evidence and the views of others, or without such attention. There are many other ways we evaluate beliefs and advise others (and ourselves) about the proper way to go about believing and disbelieving.

That means that the subject matter of epistemology is broader than the study of knowledge and its components. I think that the most general way to characterize epistemology is this: *Epistemology is the study of right or good ways to cognitively grasp reality*. When we think of epistemology that way, it naturally leads us to think about the connection between what we should believe and the other *shoulds* that apply to us, such as what we should do and what we should feel. We might also ask about the connection between what and how we *should* believe and what we should do to live an epistemically *good* life. The connection between the should and the good is one of the most fundamental issues in ethical theory, and the same issue appears in epistemology in the connection between epistemic should and epistemic good. There is also the issue of how epistemic goods such as knowledge, understanding, certainty, reasonableness, and intellectual virtue are related to the other goods that make up a good life. We will look at that question in the last chapter, but in this chapter we will start with something uncontroversial: We all care about many things. Some things are important to us and others are not. In the next section I want to argue that if we care about anything, we must care about the right way to believe. Caring about anything commits us to believing and disbelieving as we should.

II. EPISTEMIC DEMANDS AND WHAT WE CARE ABOUT

We all care about a lot of things. Even if it were possible not to care about anything, we would not have a good life if we did not care. Caring about many things is not only natural, but is part of any life we would care to live. But if we care about anything, we must care about having true beliefs in the domains we care about. If I care about my children's lives and I am minimally rational, I must care about having true beliefs about my children's lives.[3] If I care about football, I must care about having true beliefs about football. I'll call a belief that is governed by a concern for truth a **conscientiously** held belief. I assume that conscientiousness is something that comes in degrees, and I propose that (with some qualifications) the more we care about something, the more conscientious we must be.

I think that caring imposes a demand for conscientious belief on us in two ways. First, there is a demand to be conscientious in whatever beliefs we have in that domain, and second, there is a demand to acquire conscientious beliefs in the domain. The first demand is no doubt stronger than the second because our ability to care probably extends beyond our ability to form beliefs, although our inability to form beliefs in some domain probably limits our ability to care. For example, we may care about the personal

---

[3] A similar point is made by Hilary Kornblith (1993). For a more detailed argument see my essay, "Epistemic Value and the Primacy of What We Care About," Zagzebski (2004b).

well-being of all the victims of a hurricane, but since there are so many of them, none of us can acquire beliefs about very many of those people. I suspect that this limits our ability to care about them individually. What we tend to do is get beliefs about them as a class, and if that is all we have, then I suspect that we can only care about them as a class. That is probably why photojournalists try to put a face on disastrous events; it aids us in caring about the victims as individuals.

I am suggesting, then, that not only do we commit ourselves to conscientiously getting beliefs about those things we care about, but if we don't or can't do it, that tends to weaken our caring. And if we need to care about many things to have a good life, the limitations of our ability to form beliefs conscientiously limit the desirability of our lives.

There are some qualifications on the demand to acquire beliefs in the domains we care about. Sometimes having beliefs in a domain we care about conflicts with something else we care about. Even if you care about your friends' personal happiness, if you also care about their privacy, you will not care about having beliefs about the most personal aspects of their lives, at least not many detailed beliefs. So there are exceptions to the demand to conscientiously acquire beliefs in the domains of what we care about, but the exceptions also arise from something we care about, such as the privacy of other people. (This is one reason why curiosity can be a vice.)

Another qualification is that the desire to acquire beliefs about what we care about can sometimes be counterproductive. For example, health is clearly an important component of a desirable life, but obsession with one's health can detract from the desirability of one's life because getting too much information about health can impair your health. But aside from these qualifications, I think that in general, if we care about something, merely being conscientious in whatever beliefs we happen to have in that domain is not enough. We also need to get beliefs in those domains.

So we care about many things, and caring about anything imposes a demand on us to care about true belief in the domains of what we care about, and that includes a demand to acquire beliefs conscientiously in those domains. But the logic of caring demands something more than conscientious belief for a variety of reasons. For one thing, we are often agents in the domains of what we care about. We want beliefs that can serve as the ground of action, and that requires not only true beliefs, but confidence that the particular beliefs we are acting upon are true. The degree of confidence needed varies with the context. Acting involves time, usually effort, and sometimes risk or sacrifice, and it is not rational to engage in action without a degree of confidence in the truth of the beliefs upon which we act that is high enough to make the time, effort, and risk involved in acting worthwhile. Sometimes the degree of confidence we need amounts to certainty, but usually it does not.

We also know that we have false beliefs, if for no other reason than that we sometimes have beliefs that conflict, and since we do not want false beliefs in the domains of what we care about, we want mechanisms to sort out the false beliefs from the true ones. Imagine you are digging for a precious substance such as gold. (Ignore the fact that these days you are not likely to find any.) Suppose that as you dig for gold, you find lots of gold nuggets, but you also find lots of Fool's Gold, which we will imagine is hard to distinguish from real gold. Imagine also that you discover that some of the nuggets you have kept in the past are actually Fool's Gold, so even though you are pretty sure that you have lots of real gold, you are not sure which is which. Even though you have some valuable gold, it is not very helpful to have it if it is mixed up with Fool's Gold. You not only want gold, but you also want to distinguish the real gold from the fake gold. Similarly, we not only want true beliefs, but we also want to distinguish the true beliefs from the false ones. It diminishes the value of our true beliefs if they are mixed up with too many false beliefs.

Among the things we care about is caring that others care about what we care about, which means that we care about their having true beliefs about what we care about, and we also care to some extent about what they care about. So we care about being good informants to others. We want the ability to convey true beliefs and not false beliefs to others.

Conscientiousness requires self-trust. Being conscientious is all I can do to get true beliefs, but there is no guarantee that being conscientious gives me the truth. I can be careful, be thorough in seeking and evaluating evidence, be open-minded, listen to those with a contrary view, and so forth, but there are no guarantees. So I need trust that there is a close connection between conscientious belief and true belief. If I did not trust, and my lack of trust led me to have fewer conscientious beliefs in the domains I care about, I would care less about what I care about and that would give me a less desirable life, a life I would not care to have. Furthermore, since

I depend upon other people for most of my beliefs, I need another sort of trust. I am not often in a position to confirm that other people are conscientious, so I need to trust that they are. And again, if I don't trust them, I will have fewer beliefs about what I care about and that will give me a less desirable life.

The logic of caring requires that we live in a community of epistemic trust, the importance of which is dramatically described in the Greek legend of Cassandra. According to that myth, Apollo gave Cassandra the gift of prophecy as part of a scheme to seduce her. When she rebuffed him, he did not take back his gift, but did something much worse. He allowed her to continue to see the future, but she was fated never to be believed. Cassandra's curse meant that her warning that the Trojan horse was a trick went unheeded, with disastrous results for the Trojans, but its effect on her was terrible in a different way. She was the ultimate voiceless woman. Aeschylus tells us it drove her mad.[4]

Cassandra was disbelieved only in her predictions about the future, but imagine what it would be like to be disbelieved about everything you say. You would be epistemically isolated in such an extreme way that you would probably be isolated in every other way as well. Every attempt at communication would be futile, so there would be no point in trying to talk with anybody about anything.[5] You could not make plans with others, successfully express your feelings to them, or even do the minimum that it takes to carry on practical life. We need trust, but trust breaks down when people are thought to be untrustworthy. Living in a community of epistemically trusting and trustworthy people is an important requirement of any worthwhile life.

Another thing we care about is not being surprised at what happens next. We want to be able to predict the way the world will be tomorrow. We probably want that anyway, but we certainly want to be able to predict the way the world will be in ways that impinge on what we care about. That is one reason science has so much status. It allows us to explain the future as well as the past.

---

[4] In Aeschylus's play *Agamemnon*, Cassandra foresees, but can do nothing to prevent, her own death.

[5] One would expect Cassandra to give up eventually, but the mythical Cassandra never stops uttering her prophecies. The idea presumably is that truth has an authority that demands utterance. It does not go away when people don't listen. For a discussion of the relevance of the Cassandra myth to epistemic trust, see Zagzebski (2003a).

I have mentioned a series of epistemic values that we have because we care about many things and caring about things is part of living a life we would care to live. These values include true belief, the ability to distinguish true from false belief, certainty or at least confidence in our beliefs, credibility, trust and trustworthiness, and predictability. Each of these things is desirable within a domain of what we care about because we care about that domain. Caring imposes these demands on us, which means we impose these demands on ourselves by caring. Some of these values may be components of knowledge, but knowledge might be something else. In any case, knowledge also is something we want in the domains of what we care about, and we might also want knowledge for its own sake.

III. MORALITY AND EPISTEMIC DEMANDS

I have argued that even if it is optional that we care about something, what is not optional is that given that we care about it, we must care about true beliefs in that domain. But some carings themselves are not optional and I assume that caring about morality is one of them. Morality may even be in a more special category than the nonoptional because there are things all persons should care about, such as health, yet people may permissibly and even admirably negotiate their health against other goods, as when a person sacrifices her health for the life or freedom of others. That may mean that even though health is something we should all care about, it is not something we must care about absolutely. Morality is different because it is both nonoptional and is not something we may trade off for other values. We do not get to exchange moral values for nonmoral values. For example, we don't get to decide to violate the obligations of our roles as parents or teachers for something we personally value but which is optional.[6]

If morality's importance to us is not optional, it follows that conscientious belief in the domain of morality is not optional either. Morality puts a demand on us to be epistemically conscientious in

---

[6] An interesting suggestion to the contrary is Bernard Williams's well-known example of Gauguin, who left his family in France to go to Tahiti and paint. Williams says we might excuse the immorality because of the great artistic value of Gauguin's paintings. See his essay "Moral Luck" in Williams (1981).

beliefs relevant to morality and moral decision-making. There is a moral demand not to violate any epistemic demands. It is morally wrong to be epistemically unconscientious in any of these beliefs. Some things are morally more important than others, so the degree of the conscientiousness demanded of us by morality varies.

This means that I must care about identifying the beliefs relevant to the domain of morality. Suppose that I do not know much about global warming, but I do care about morality. One of the things demanded of me by morality is caring about what is a moral matter and what is not. So morality demands that I be epistemically conscientious in seeking beliefs that pertain to morality. If an epistemically conscientious search for such beliefs would lead me to acquire beliefs about global warming, then there is a moral demand on me to acquire epistemically conscientious beliefs about global warming.

I think, though, that we need to be careful not to exaggerate the level of demand on each individual. Global warming may be a moral issue and an important one to us taken collectively, but it does not follow that its level of moral importance to every individual is great. Global warming is an issue in which everyone has a shared interest, unlike the safety of my children, where I am one of only two people who have the special interest of a parent. I may be conscientious enough to satisfy the demands of morality if I accept what I read or hear from those I trust about global warming, whereas the same level of conscientiousness might be insufficient if the safety of my children were threatened. And the demand to acquire beliefs relevant to the safety of my children (at least while they are young and in my care) no doubt greatly exceeds the demand on me to acquire beliefs relevant to global warming. So in the domain of my children's safety, both the degree of the demand on me to be conscientious and the degree of the conscientiousness demanded is greater than in the domain of global warming.

These considerations about the demands of what we care about can explain what is right about a famous example given by W. K. Clifford in his landmark essay, "The Ethics of Belief."[7] Clifford describes a ship owner who sends his ship full of emigrants to sea, believing without evidence that his ship is seaworthy. When the ship goes down, Clifford is surely right that the ship owner is morally

---

[7] The essay is found in Clifford Stephen, and Pollock. (1901), although it has also been reprinted in many anthologies.

wrong in being epistemically unconscientious, but Clifford uses this example to support his thesis that it is morally wrong for *anyone* to believe *anything* upon insufficient evidence. According to Clifford, every belief is a moral matter, and the standards for conscientious belief are equally severe. Furthermore, Clifford thinks that conscientious believing is a matter of basing one's belief on evidence, the view usually called **evidentialism**. But if I'm right in the account I've given of the relationship between caring and epistemic demands, Clifford both overstates the connection between morality and evidence and misses the moral relevance of aspects of conscientiousness other than the weighing of evidence.

For one thing, the moral demand on the ship owner to be conscientious in his belief depends upon the context. Suppose that the ship owner has no intentions of sending the ship to sea, but if he can attest that the ship is seaworthy, he will get a tax deduction. He believes the ship is seaworthy and declares that it is in order to get the deduction, but does not bother to do a careful inspection of the ship. He may be morally guilty for violating an epistemic norm, but his wrongdoing is far less than in Clifford's case because the demand on him is less. Or maybe he simply announces to a friend that his ship is seaworthy while the two of them are in a bar, bragging to each other about their respective ships. At worst he has violated a weak moral requirement.

Clifford misses the importance of context, but he also misses the moral importance of epistemic goods other than evidence. In Ian McEwan's novel *Atonement* (2002), a bright and imaginative thirteen-year-old girl, Briony Tallis, witnesses a flirtatious incident between her older sister, Cecilia, and Robbie Turner, the talented son of a servant, who has been awarded a scholarship to Cambridge. When Briony later finds them in an embrace, her sexual innocence combined with her attraction to the melodramatic leads her to interpret the event as an act of aggression against her sister. When a guest is raped later that night in the dark wood near the house, Briony, who had a fleeting glimpse of the assailant, swears that it was Robbie. The innocent Robbie is convicted and sent to prison upon Briony's evidence, breaking the family apart and ruining the lives of Robbie and Cecilia. In this story, Briony sincerely believes her testimony, but her belief is acquired unconscientiously and is a moral wrong to Robbie and others. The adults in the story also form beliefs and act upon their beliefs unconscientiously, and we probably blame them more than Briony, since the demands of conscientiousness in adults no doubt exceed the demands on children.

This story illustrates the moral obligation to care about true belief, but in addition, it shows the moral demand to care about some of the other epistemic goods mentioned earlier—trustworthiness, credibility, knowledge, and understanding—and it shows the moral importance of such intellectual virtues as carefulness, open-mindedness, intellectual fairness, and intellectual humility, which go well beyond Clifford's demand to have sufficient evidence. But it also supports another point Clifford makes, which is that the great wrong of believing unconscientiously is that it becomes a habit and makes a person credulous. Briony's personality and the isolated circumstances of her life make her a credulous person. In this case the results are tragic, but Clifford is right that intellectual credulity is a moral failing whether or not it has tragic results.

Of course there are many beliefs we will never act upon and neither will anybody else, so a failure of conscientiousness in these beliefs does not seem to be a moral failing. But what is disturbing about lack of conscientiousness is that it becomes a habit, and once a person has that habit, it is unlikely she can limit her acting on that habit to the domain of the trivial. If we have the habit of believing unconscientiously, given that we care about lots of things, we are unlikely to escape acting immorally by hurting other people, and we are also unlikely to escape acting against our own commitments to what we care about.

William James gave a famous objection to Clifford is his essay "The Will to Believe."[8] James observed that the passion to get truth and the passion to avoid falsehood are two distinct passions, and they lead to different strategies. The passion to get truth leads to more risk-taking than the passion to avoid falsehood, which leads to a more conservative strategy. One can ensure that one has no false beliefs by believing very few things and making sure that what one does believe satisfies the most stringent standards; but in doing so, one not only avoids false beliefs, one also foregoes many true beliefs. The passion to get truth, in contrast, will lead one to have more beliefs, some of which may be false. The standards of the person dominated by the passion for truth will be somewhat looser than the standards of the

---

[8] See James (1979). James's essay, like Clifford's, has been reprinted in numerous anthologies.

person dominated by the passion to avoid falsehood. Clifford's evidentialist principle arises out of the passion to avoid falsehood rather than the passion to get truth. It is a principle of safety. James thinks that the passion to get truth is as rational as the passion to avoid falsehood. Reason cannot determine which passion should dominate, since both are, after all, passions. I would think that the conscientious believer is driven by both passions. Neither should dictate one's entire belief-forming life, but it is not irrational for one of them to be more important than the other.

Earlier I mentioned that I think conscientiousness in belief has two aspects. First, there is a demand to be conscientious in whatever beliefs we have in the domains we care about, and second, there is a demand to acquire conscientious beliefs in those domains. But these demands can pull us in opposing directions. James's point about the two epistemic passions is related to the two requirements of conscientiousness. The requirement that we be conscientious in the beliefs we have is a principle of safety. Even if the principle is not interpreted as stringently as Clifford's evidentialist principle, it is a principle that is aimed at ensuring that each and every belief we have is formed and maintained with an eye to the likelihood that given the other beliefs we have, this one is likely to be true. This is a principle of caution. The second requirement that we obtain beliefs in the areas we care about is a principle of risk, of taking chances on getting the truth that we want. It is the principle that tells us that we cannot succeed if we do not try. We risk the failure of falsehood, but we also get the chance of success.

I think we need to be aware that the two demands of conscientiousness pull us in opposing directions. If we are too careful in our beliefs, we may end up not having enough true beliefs about important matters to lead a good life. For example, it seems to me that the following questions are important:

> Is there a God? Is there purpose in the universe? Does the life of an individual human being have the special value Kant called a dignity? If so, what is the source of that value? Do human beings have free will? Is a human being the same thing as a physical body? What makes one life more admirable than another? What kind of life should I wish for my children?

Answers to these questions can be conscientiously held, but if our standards for conscientiousness are as stringent as Clifford's, agnosticism about most of these questions would probably follow. On the other hand, Clifford is right that we need caution because beliefs can be dangerous to ourselves and to others. We want to avoid both ignorance about important matters and error about such matters. It is not at all obvious how to balance the two strategies.

Simon Blackburn is a prominent contemporary defender of Clifford who has strongly defended our duty to reason. Unfortunately, Blackburn (2005) is moved to say the following:

> Clifford is right. Someone sitting on a completely unreasonable belief is sitting on a time bomb. The apparently harmless, idiosyncratic belief of the Catholic Church that one thing may have the same substance as another, although it displays absolutely none of its empirical qualities, prepares people for the view that some people are agents of Satan in disguise, which in turn makes it reasonable to destroy them. (p. 5)

It is obvious that a conscientious believer can believe in the doctrine of transubstantiation and have no inclination to think that people are agents of Satan whom one ought to destroy, nor need they have the habit of forming irrational beliefs in general. One wonders if Blackburn's passion is about something other than evidence. However, Blackburn is right that acts can be morally unjustified at least partly *because* they are based on epistemically unjustified beliefs. If I attack my new next-door neighbor when he comes to my door to meet me because I believe he has a hidden weapon and has come to kill me, you will think the act and the belief are both crazy, but the *connection* between the act and the belief may not be crazy. In fact, it may be quite reasonable. If I were fully conscientious in my belief about the intent of my neighbor, my act might be justified. Assuming it is not justified, I have already gone wrong morally as soon as I have the belief.

The range of beliefs that must be epistemically conscientious as a demand of morality is probably very wide. It is not at all obvious whether some belief will be relevant to moral judgment or action by myself or someone else who relies on my testimony, so that gives me a prima facie duty to be conscientious in a vast number of my beliefs. When we add to that the range of things I care about outside of morality, including caring about what others care about, that broadens even more the range of beliefs that I am required to be epistemically justified in holding. Finally, there are epistemic demands of social roles. A jurist in a litigation case has an obligation to reach a decision conscientiously whether or not she cares about the case and whether or not the case involves something within the domain of morality. Here the epistemic demand arises not from what she cares about personally, but from the importance of the role itself.

It follows from what I've said in the last two sections that we commit ourselves to following epistemic norms by being human. Morality, our social roles, and the many things we personally care about all put epistemic demands on us that apply to almost everything we believe as well as many things we do not believe but should believe. The issues discussed in this book are not merely of academic interest, but apply to the way we all should conduct our lives.

IV. BULLSHIT

Since we depend upon each other for information as well as much else that we need to live a worthwhile life, we want to be good informants, and we want others to be good informants to us. So there are norms governing what we say to each other as well as what we believe. What we say usually has a greater impact on other people than what we believe, but less of an impact than what we do.

We would expect, then, that the ethics of what we say is in between the ethics of belief and the ethics of action. I have already argued that there are moral demands on us to be epistemically conscientious, but in our society people can get away with believing anything for any reason, and they can get away with saying almost anything for any reason. The exceptions usually involve racist speech or speech directed at particular ethnic or religious groups. But it is not the epistemic impropriety that is typically the object of censure. People complain when words become a form of assault. However, if I am right that caring about anything requires us to care about truth in the domains of what we care about, that would apply to what we say as well as to what we believe. The basic rule of assertion, I propose, is that we speak with a conscientious regard for the truth. There are no doubt secondary rules of assertion that follow from that, as well as rules that follow from the other epistemic values mentioned earlier, but I'm only going to talk about the basic one.

Of course, there are uses of speech in which the truth does not matter. Jokes are an obvious example, but jokes are cases in which all parties know that the usual rules of assertion are on hold.[9] Another situation in which the rules may not hold occurs when the speaker prefaces her assertion by saying something like, "It's just my opinion, but . . . ." I suspect that this remark serves a very important purpose in communication. It alerts the hearer that the speaker does not want to be held to the usual rules of assertion. The speaker may not be sure that what she is saying arises from a conscientious regard for the truth, or perhaps she thinks it does, but she does not want to be held accountable to others for doing so. Saying that something is just her opinion protects her from the kind of criticism to which we are liable when we do not follow the rules of assertion but pretend that we are.

So aside from situations in which the rules of assertion are set aside, the primary rule is that we speak out of a concern to express the truth. This brings us to Harry Frankfurt's popular book, *On Bullshit* (2005). What Frankfurt means by bullshit is speech that does not show a proper concern for the truth (p. 47). According to Frankfurt, there is lots and lots of bullshit and we are all responsible for our share. What is wrong with it, he says, is not that it is false, but that the bullshitter misrepresents what he is up to (p. 54). An implied rule of communication is that you say what you have good reason to believe is true, and the bullshitter pretends to follow the rules, but does not. Such a person is faking.

Frankfurt is disturbed that people simply get impatient or pass off BS with an irritated shrug, reacting more strongly to lies (p. 50). Frankfurt thinks that this is a mistake because what is really bad about bullshit is that it unfits a person for telling the truth. The liar, in contrast, is quite capable of telling the truth; he simply chooses not to. The liar and the truth-teller are playing on opposite sides of the same game. The bullshitter is playing a different game but represents himself as playing the same game. The bullshitter is worse than the liar because if bullshitting becomes a habit, he loses the capacity to say what he really thinks is the case (p. 60).

Frankfurt says bullshit is inevitable whenever people are required by circumstances to speak about something without knowing what they're talking about, which is why it is so common in public life, and, I would add, among teachers. Frankfurt says there are also

---

[9] Sometimes jokes have a serious side to them and are an indirect way of saying something. This feature of jokes can put the listener in an awkward position because she might reject what is implied in a joke, but there is nothing for her to respond to, since the joker has not actually asserted anything. I think this happens frequently with political jokes.

pressures to bullshit when citizens are expected to have opinions about everything they will vote about, and I have noticed that we are often asked our opinions about anything that appears in the news, including subjects that require special expertise, such as stem cell research, the consequences of various medical insurance proposals, and local politics in the Middle East. At the worst, Frankfurt says, bullshit undermines confidence that there is such a thing as objective truth. When that happens, there is a shift from the ideal of truth-telling to the ideal of sincerity—the accurate representation of oneself, rather than the accurate representation of what we take reality to be. If you are convinced that reality outside yourself has no determinate nature that you can hope to truthfully represent, then you aim only at truthfully representing yourself. But Frankfurt says it is preposterous to think that the self has a determinate nature while everything else does not. We cannot know ourselves without knowing the world outside ourselves. He concludes that sincerity is bullshit.

I think this is right as far as it goes. What I have added is a reason why we should care that others fake a concern for truth. The problem is not only that we don't like faking. Since we commit ourselves to care about truth if we care about anything, bullshit goes directly against the things we care about. Most of what we believe comes from others, so we must trust that others are conscientious in what they tell us. But if somebody bullshits, either I recognize it as bullshit or I don't. Suppose first that I don't. I trust the bullshitter and believe what he says, and let's suppose that I am doing that conscientiously. That is, it isn't my fault that I don't recognize that he is not trustworthy. In that case, the desirability of my life is undermined because there is now a weaker connection between my believing conscientiously and getting the truth. On the other hand, suppose that I recognize the bullshitter for what he is and I don't trust what he says. In that case the desirability of my life is undermined in a different way because he prevents me from getting conscientiously acquired beliefs in a domain I care about. So whether or not I believe him, I am harmed.

Suppose I try to avoid the problem by ceasing to care about what-ever the BSer is talking about. That won't save the desirability of my life either. For one thing, we can't just decide to stop caring about things we care about, but even if we could, we wouldn't have a desirable life if we were forced to stop caring because of the untrustworthiness of others. If we stop caring about every domain in which our primary sources of information cannot be trusted, we will end up caring about much less than we would if there wasn't so much bullshit in the world. And if I'm right that a desirable life requires caring about many things, then ceasing to care leads to a less desirable life. I conclude that any way you look at it, bullshit undermines a desirable life for others, and since the perpetrator of BS cannot trust himself, it undermines what he cares about, and so it undermines the desirability of his own life.

Bullshit is connected with hypocrisy in a way I find interesting. Both are a kind of bluffing. Frankfurt does not mention hypocrisy, but it is curious that whereas bullshit is often tolerated, as Frankfurt notes, people get hysterical over hypocrisy. In fact, until terrorism got so much public attention, hypocrisy was virtually the only vice publicly repudiated. Cowardice, sexual immorality, dishonesty, and even murder are often tolerated, even defended, but the scorn heaped upon hypocrisy goes way beyond the bounds of any other moral criticism, and people claim to see hypocrisy everywhere, particularly in public officials. The hypocrite is someone who wants people to think he is a morally admirable person when he is not.[10] The bullshitter wants people to think he cares about the truth when he does not. Frankfurt says that the person who bullshits is not concerned with the truth; he is concerned with what other people think of *him*. I'm not sure I agree that the bullshitter is always concerned with how he or she appears to others. Since having a regard for the truth takes some discipline, he might just be lazy. Still, I imagine that a significant number of bullshitters are motivated by the same thing that motivates the hypocrite.

But now I would like to leave the reader with a puzzle. It seems to me that people get away with bullshit unless others don't like them to begin with, whereas people are oversensitive to hypocrisy, roundly condemning it and claiming to see it everywhere. I suspect that people *like* the idea that certain other people are hypocrites, whereas there is nothing particularly enjoyable about the idea that other people bullshit.[11]

---

[10] I think that many people confuse hypocrisy with other moral failings such as weakness of will, what the Greeks called *akrasia*. That occurs when a person violates moral norms she herself accepts. Knowing the right thing to do but not doing it is so common it hardly needs comment. But mere weakness is not hypocrisy. It is just moral failure.

[11] When William Bennett, the author of *The Book of Virtues*, was revealed to be a high-stakes gambler, many people accused him of hypocrisy and seemed to enjoy the idea that he is a hypocrite. I don't know the man, but from what I have read, he never pretended to be a nongambler. Gambling is against neither the teachings of his Church (Catholic) nor his personal beliefs. Furthermore, his income was high enough to pay his debts, and his family did not suffer. I see no evidence that he is a hypocrite, but plenty of evidence that people want him to be a hypocrite. Al Gore may be another example of a person whom many people want to be a hypocrite.

V. SKEPTICISM AND WHAT WE CARE ABOUT

In this chapter I have argued that epistemology is the study of the things we care about in our beliefs and the ways we commit ourselves to believe because of other things we care about. So an important object of epistemological inquiry is conscientious belief. Since many of our beliefs come from other people, we care about the conscientiousness of their beliefs also. We would not want to live in a world where people are careless about the truth concerning things we care about. That means we are committed to caring about lies and bullshit. We hate to be misled and we hate to be fooled.

If we were living in a virtual reality machine, we would be fooled in a big way. We probably all believe that we are not living in a virtual reality machine, but we want to be conscientious in *that* belief too. If what I've said about the connection between caring and conscientiousness is correct, we commit ourselves to being conscientious in that belief. The more important it is to us that we are not living in a virtual reality machine, the more conscientious we must be in believing we are not. The degree of the demand to be conscientious depends upon the level at which we care. That follows from the logic of caring, whether or not it has anything to do with knowledge. Philosophers probably care more than the average person, and that is one of the reasons skepticism is much more threatening to philosophers than to other people. It is not the awareness of the possibility of the skeptical scenario itself that is the problem, but caring about the way the world would be if the possibility obtained. In my opinion skepticism is hard to understand without this link to what we care about.

As we will see in the next two chapters, skepticism is often interpreted as a threat to knowledge, and it disappears once we have an account of knowledge according to which we know we are not a brain in a vat. But unfortunately, the threat to knowledge is only one of the problems of skepticism. Skepticism is a threat to conscientious belief, and we may quite rightly fear that there is something wrong with permitting looser standards for the conscientiousness of the belief that we are not living in a skeptical scenario while simultaneously expecting higher standards for our beliefs about matters about which we care much less. To take an example at random, are we justified in having stringent standards for beliefs about the health dangers of various foods while permitting ourselves looser standards for the belief that we are not living in a virtual reality machine? In the next two chapters we will look carefully at skepticism and a host of responses to it. A number of major issues in the history of epistemology in the last half century will be included in this discussion.

FURTHER READING

There are many introductory texts in epistemology, as well as anthologies that students at all levels will find useful. For an encyclopedic collection of essays, see *A Companion to Epistemology*, edited by Jonathan Dancy and Ernest Sosa (Oxford: Blackwell, 1992). Robert Audi's classic text *Epistemology: A Contemporary Introduction to the Theory of Knowledge* (New York: Routledge, 2003) engages the reader to "practice" epistemology instead of merely informing students about it. Laurence BonJour's *Epistemology: Classic Problems and Contemporary Responses* (Lanham, MD: Rowman & Littlefield, 2002) begins with a large section devoted to surveying epistemological problems that arose in the modern period. For a straightforward introduction, students may want to read Richard Feldman, *Epistemology* (Upper Saddle River, NJ: Prentice Hall, 2003), or Richard Fumerton, *Epistemology* (Malden, MA: Blackwell Publishing, 2006). Louis P. Pojman's *The Theory of Knowledge: Classical and Contemporary Readings* (Belmont, CA: Wadsworth Publishing Co., 2002) is a collection of ancient, modern, and twentieth-century contributions. John Greco and Ernest Sosa (eds.), *The Blackwell Guide to Epistemology* (Malden, MA: Blackwell Publishing, 1999), is another large collection containing essays by contemporary epistemologists on a range of topics. For current issues, see *Contemporary Debates in Epistemology*, edited by Matthias Steup and Ernest Sosa (Oxford: Blackwell Publishing, 2005), which presents opposing positions on recent topics of debate in epistemology.

2

Skepticism and Some Contemporary Responses

I. INTRODUCTION

Skepticism is an instance of a general problem of the human condition. We often try to reach goals without a guarantee that success is within our reach, and sometimes without even a guarantee that we will ever find out whether or not we succeeded. This phenomenon occurs in our practical life, but we call it skepticism when it occurs in our attempts to get true belief, knowledge, or any other distinctively epistemic good. There is even a form of skepticism about understanding, although philosophers rarely mention that problem. Skepticism is almost always treated as applying to true belief, knowledge, or justified belief. So we can try but fail in getting the truth, a justified belief, or knowledge and never discover our failure.

There are many degrees and kinds of skepticism. Most of us adopt some degree of skepticism about our own memory, and we may be somewhat skeptical of our sense experience (although not as much as we should be).[1] If Frankfurt is right about the prevalence of bullshit, we should adopt some degree of skepticism about other people's assertions, and there are further grounds for skepticism about the assertions of others, given that even when people do not bullshit, they often lie or are simply mistaken.

---

[1] Legal experts say that the least reliable form of testimony in a court of law is the eyewitness account, and juries tend to put much more credence in this form of testimony than is justified. See Loftus (1996) for an interesting book reviewing problems with eyewitness testimony.

Hume's famous skeptical attack on induction is the problem that we cannot justifiably conclude anything about the future based on observations about the past without making the assumption that the future will be like the past, yet how could we defend that assumption without using induction? We could say that *past* futures have been like *past* pasts, but that does not help, because we cannot conclude that the relation between future futures and future pasts will be like that between past futures and past pasts without the assumption that the future will be like the past. Skepticism about induction threatens many of our belief-forming procedures, both in our practical life and in science.

There is also widespread skepticism about answers to philosophical questions. Some of these answers and the questions they answer are so rarified that only a few people pay any attention to them, for example, is Abelard's love of Heloise an exemplification of the universal Love, or a particular bit of the property Love (a so-called trope)? But other questions are the object of basic human concern, such as the existence of free will. Do we have any guarantee that our belief in free will is true? Do we know that we have free will? Is the belief justified? Many philosophers think that the answer to some or all of these questions is no, yet they continue to believe in free will. In fact, Peter van Inwagen claims that everyone implicitly believes they have free will in the sense of the ability to do otherwise even though some philosophers also believe (or claim to believe) that they do not. (Their beliefs are therefore contradictory.) But van Inwagen (2000) calls free will a mystery because we cannot see how to justify our belief in it.

Perhaps the existence of free will is an example of something we believe, but don't know, and we know we don't know it. Many other metaphysical beliefs may be in this category, such as beliefs about immortality, the explanation for evil, or the belief that another person feels the same thing you feel when both of you cut your finger with a knife. Even worse, there are things that we don't know, but we are unaware that we don't know them.[2] Radical skeptical hypotheses

---

[2] Comedians and journalists had a field day when former Secretary of Defense Donald Rumsfeld made the following comments during a press conference:

> Reports that say that something hasn't happened are always interesting to me, because as we know, there are known knowns; there are things we know we know. We also know there are known unknowns; that is to say we know there are some things we do not know. But there are also unknown unknowns—the ones we don't know we don't know.

The Plain English Campaign even selected his comment for its 2003 "Foot in Mouth" Award, an annual award that highlights "a baffling comment made by a public figure." But most philosophers did not find Rumsfeld's comment baffling.

purport to show that most of our beliefs are in this category. If we were all living in a virtual reality machine, presumably we would have no way to find out we were living in such a machine. Most of our beliefs would be false, and hence, not knowledge. And even if we are not living in a virtual reality machine and most of our beliefs are true, they still may fail to be knowledge if we are not justified or conscientious in believing we are not living in the machine. So we would not know that there are table and chairs in the room, yet most of us would not know that we do not know such things when we do not. Arguably, this would be a worse kind of skepticism than skepticism about free will or immortality because a person typically would be in the following situation with respect to belief in free will:

Situation 1

(a) She believes she has free will.

(b) She does not know she has free will.

(c) She knows she does not know she has free will.

In contrast, the possibility that she is living in a virtual reality machine puts her in the following situation with respect to most of her beliefs about the world around her and her own body:

Situation 2

(d) She believes she is sitting on a chair.

(e) She does not know she is sitting on a chair.

(f) She does not know that she does not know she is sitting on a chair.

I assume that situation 2 is worse than situation 1, although I have noticed individual differences in response. Some students say that situation 2 is not as bad as situation 1 because "Ignorance is bliss," "What you don't know can't hurt you," and so forth. I find situation 2 worse for roughly the reasons I gave at the end of Chapter One. I *care* that the world is more or less the way I think it is. If it were not, I would be cheated, and I would be cheated even if I didn't know I was cheated. In fact, if I believed that I knew that I was sitting on a chair, I would be doubly cheated: cheated in what I believe about the world, and cheated in what I believe about my beliefs.

Now the shrewd reader may notice something interesting about the skeptical hypothesis and comparing situations 1 and 2. Arguably, once you think of the possibility that you are living in a virtual reality machine, you are no longer in situation 2. You may move into situation 1 as soon as you think about the argument in the paragraph above. Again, whether that counts as progress depends upon what you care about. But there is an oddity about situation 1 that is worth mentioning, and that is that you couldn't be in situation 1 about *all* of your beliefs. If you were, you would have to know that you don't know anything, but that, of course, is impossible.

Ever since Descartes, radical skeptical hypotheses in which we are living in a virtual reality machine or are fooled by an evil but god-like genius get the most attention in discussions of skepticism, but there are other sources of skeptical doubt that are much more ancient. One of them is the Infinite Regress Argument, the topic of the next section. This problem is not based on what many people consider far-fetched possibilities such as being a Brain in a Vat or being fooled by Descartes's Evil Genius. The basic assumption is something that many philosophers consider obviously true: A belief must be justified in order to be a case of knowledge. But that assumption leads directly to a skeptical conclusion, as we will see in the next section.

In the rest of this chapter and the next, I will present three "stages" of the skeptical attack. Although I think the first stage is historically more ancient than the other two, I am not presenting them in this order because of their chronology, but because I think they represent three degrees of skeptical worry, from least to most threatening. I am not confident that I am right about their relative importance, but that probably does not matter since all of them are threatening enough to deserve attention, and indeed, much of the history of modern philosophy can be read as ways of getting out of these three types of skeptical argument. I will include contemporary replies to the first two skeptical arguments in this chapter. In Chapter Three I will turn to a metaphysical form of the skeptical problem and a different kind of response.

II. THE FIRST STAGE OF THE SKEPTICAL ATTACK: THE INFINITE REGRESS OF REASONS

A. Pyrrhonism and the Regress

Skepticism in ancient Greece lasted for many centuries, beginning with Pyrrho of Ellis (365–270 B.C.) who lived in the generation after Aristotle. Either Pyrrho did not write anything, or his writings have been lost, and most of what we know about Pyrrhonism comes from later followers, particularly Sextus Empiricus, who wrote about five hundred years later. Sextus collected the views of his predecessors on the various modes of inquiry and it is unclear how much of his work is original. After the decline of Pyrrhonian skepticism, it was treated as a historical curiosity and was not considered philosophically important for many centuries.

Recently, there has been a lot of interest in this form of skepticism and some philosophers think it is a more significant threat to the possibility of knowledge than the skepticism of Descartes, which we will examine in sections III and IV.[3] This is for at least two reasons, one of which I have already mentioned. Pyrrhonian skepticism is not based on the apparently outlandish possibility of being fooled about all of our experience by an Evil Genius, and it does not presuppose that you don't know unless you have certainty. The standards for knowledge presupposed by the Pyrrhonists are quite ordinary. They argued that all a person needs for a justified belief is that the evidence for some proposition believed exceeds the evidence against it, no matter by how little, and they argued that skepticism follows from this quite reasonable assumption. Their arguments do not depend upon an excessively rigorous standard for knowledge.

Furthermore, they did not present their skeptical challenge as an argument with premises and a conclusion. They claimed that philosophy is a sort of therapy that automatically leads to a skeptical suspension of belief when you go through their various "modes," or considerations that lead to the suspension of belief in various categories. They did not argue that you *should* suspend belief, nor did they claim to *know* that nobody has any knowledge (the self-refuting claim mentioned above). They thought that the medicine of their skeptical modes would lead to a state they called *ataraxia* or quietude, a blissful state that relieves us of the anxiety of having to make judgments. This is not a state from which we should try to escape. On the contrary, it is a state of epistemic contentment.

The idea that the skeptical state is pleasant will seem strange to most people today. The Pyrrhonists clearly did not care if the world is much different from what it appears to be, and since they made no effort to get out of skepticism, the elaborate theories of modern philosophers to avoid skeptical conclusions would have struck them

---

[3] Peter Klein argues for the seriousness of Pyrrhonian skepticism in (1999) and (2000).

as wrong-headed. Philosophy, like everything else we do, is driven by what we care about and how much we care about it. As I've said, philosophers generally find skepticism a fearful prospect. Ironically, Pyrrhonian skepticism now enjoys a lot of attention, not because there are many people who agree with the Pyrrhonists that the goal of life is *ataraxia*, but for the opposite reason: They want to make sure they are not forced into skepticism. Philosophers find the Pyrrhonists' arguments worrisome.

The Pyrrhonists had many arguments intended to show that the evidence for some proposition *p* never exceeds the evidence against *p*. Here is a version of one Pyrrhonian argument that has shaped a great deal of later-twentieth-century epistemology.

The Regress Argument

(1) For any proposition *p*, I know *p* only if I am justified in believing *p*.

(2) I am justified in believing *p* only if I have evidence E that justifies *p*.

(3) No evidence E can justify a proposition unless E is justified.

(4) So E is justified only if there is evidence E1 that justifies E.

(5) E1 is justified only if there is evidence E2 that justifies E1.

(6) E2 is justified only if there is evidence E3 that justifies E2. ... ad infinitum.

Since the process of justification is never-ending, it follows that

(7) I am never justified in believing any proposition.

Hence, by (1) it follows

(8) I do not know anything.

The Pyrrhonists would not have given the regress argument in this form, for good reason. They did not claim to know (1), (2), or (3), and so, of course, they were not forced to make the self-refuting claim that they know (8). They began by judging (1), (2), and (3), and by the time they got to (6) or somewhere in the regress, judgments evaporated. They simply stopped making judgments. Presumably they thought that the suspension of judgment was the right response to the consideration of the infinite regress of reasons, but they did not *judge* that it was the right response. That is, they did not tell people "You should stop making judgments."[4]

Contemporary philosophers, however, want to block the Pyrrhonian medicine from taking its effect by rejecting something in the argument. Some premise is false, they argue, or maybe (7) does not follow from the previous steps. Notice first that the regress does not even get going without the assumption of premise (1) that justification is a component of knowledge, an assumption that was widely accepted in the latter part of the twentieth century, as I mentioned in Chapter One. Premise (2) affirms the evidentialist principle of Clifford, another principle widely accepted in that period. Premise (3) seems innocuous. So from the point of view of many later-twentieth-century epistemologists, there had to be some reason to block the regress leading to (7). A very large literature developed over the only two positions that were thought to block the inference to (7): **foundationalism** and **coherentism**.

How serious is the regress argument? You might be tempted to think that the farther we go back in the regress, the more justified a belief becomes, and that might lead you to conclude that even if the regress argument shows that no belief p is fully justified, it is at least partially justified as long as p is justified by E1 that is justified by E2 that is justified by E3 that is justified by E4. The longer the sequence of justifying reasons supporting p, the more justified p is.

Unfortunately, it is not at all clear that this is the right way to think about the regress. If a belief is crazy, it is no less crazy if supported by a long series of justifying reasons each of which is just as crazy. To see why, consider a belief such as the following:

(i) Evil UFOs who take over humans' minds have landed on the neighbor's roof.

---

[4] I am not sure that the Pyrrhonists never judged that one should not judge. According to Eusebius in *Praeparatio evangelica* 14.18.2–5, Pyrrho's student Timon said that "Pyrrho declared that [1] things are equally indifferent, unmeasurable and inarbitrable. For this reason [2] neither our sensations nor our opinions tell us truths or falsehoods. Therefore, for this reason we should not put our trust in them one bit, but we should be unopinionated, uncommitted and unwavering, saying concerning each individual thing that it no more is than is not, or it both is and is not, or it neither is nor is not." Here Eusebius is quoting from Aristocles who quotes Timon on Pyrrho. Obviously, this is several steps removed from Pyrrho. In any case, even if some Pyrrhonists fell into the trap of judging that one should not judge, it is pretty clear that they did not have to do that, given their views about the process of reaching *ataraxia*. It seems to me, then, that Pyrrhonian skepticism can be interpreted as a consistent position.

That belief can be used to justify

(ii) The neighbors are not human anymore in spite of appearances.

That would justify

(iii) When the neighbors speak to me, they are lying and planning something nefarious.

That would justify

(iv) If the neighbors come to the door allegedly collecting for the March of Dimes, they plan to harm me.

That in turn might justify

(v) I should shoot the neighbors when they come to the door in a pre-emptive strike against them.

Of course, (v) is unjustified, but is it any less unjustified because it is supported by a chain of evidence (i)–(iv)? Since (i) is irrational, it makes every belief that depends upon it irrational too, including (v). So the mere fact that a chain of justification is long is not sufficient to make a belief even partially justified. When we go back in our chain of justifying reasons for some belief, we never know whether we will come across a belief like (i). If we do, the whole chain of justifying reasons collapses. That suggests that a long chain of justifying reasons for some belief may be no better than no chain at all. We need to look at the entire chain in order to determine whether a given belief is justified, and unfortunately we cannot do that with an infinitely long chain.

B. Responses to the Regress: Foundationalism versus Coherentism

Foundationalism and coherentism are competing theories about the structure of a system of justified beliefs. Roughly, the foundationalist maintains that the structure of a justified or rational belief system is like a brick wall, with a few ground level beliefs that are not supported by any other beliefs, but which support all the beliefs above them. In contrast, the coherentist maintains that the structure of a justified belief system is an interlocking network of beliefs. The foundationalist ends the regress in a set of foundational beliefs, whereas the coherentist maintains that the sequence of justifying beliefs loops back upon itself. Examples of foundationalists are Roderick Chisholm,[5] Richard Feldman (2003), John Pollock (2001), and Alvin Plantinga (1993). Examples of coherentists are Paul Thagard (2000), Keith Lehrer (2000), and Laurence BonJour (until recently).[6] A third possibility that has recently emerged is the position that Peter Klein (1999) calls infinitism, according to which the infinite regress is benign and does not lead to (7).[7]

Before looking at these three positions, I think it is worth noticing an important feature of the debate among them. Both Chisholm and BonJour argue to their positions by a process of elimination. They pick the least unacceptable alternative to skepticism. Klein does the same with infinitism. I find this interesting because none of the three seems to think of his position as independently plausible. By that I mean that it is doubtful that they would come to accept their respective positions were it not for the threat of skepticism as presented in the regress argument. Some foundationalists, however, do think of their position as independently plausible. Descartes presupposes foundationalism without any mention of the regress argument, and as we will see in the next section, he thought that if foundational beliefs are certain, foundationalism has the potential to avoid another form of skepticism as well. But in this section we will look at foundationalism, coherentism, and infinitism as responses to the problem of the regress of reasons.

The foundationalist and the coherentist agree that there cannot be an infinitely long chain of justifying reasons for a belief *p*. In the first place, we do not have an infinitely long chain of reasons justifying any of our beliefs, and in the second place, even if we had an infinitely long chain of reasons, that would not be sufficient to justify the belief, so skepticism follows.

The assumption that an infinite chain of reasons does not justify a belief bears an interesting similarity to an assumption used in the simplest version of the First Cause Argument for the existence of God. According to that argument, an object caused to exist by an infinitely long chain of

---

[5] See, for example, Chisholm (1964), (1977), and (1982).

[6] BonJour defended the coherentist position in BonJour (1976) and (1978). However, more recently he has defended a form of foundationalism—see, for example, BonJour and Sosa (2003). For more on the dialectic between foundationalists and coherentists, see Pojman (2002), especially the section "Theories of Justification (I): Foundationalism and Coherentism." Susan Haack (1993) defends a mixed theory she calls "foundherentism."

[7] Other defenders of infinitism include Jeremy Fantl (2003) and Scott Aikin (2005). Historical precedent for this position can be found in the early-twentieth-century philosopher Charles Peirce (1868).

causes has no cause for its existence, so there cannot be an infinite chain of causes. In the same way, the foundationalist and coherentist argue that a belief justified by an infinitely long chain of reasons is not justified; hence, there cannot be an infinite chain of reasons. The foundationalist adds that the chain of justifying reasons cannot be circular. The intuition here is like the intuition that a chain of causes cannot be circular. The foundationalist argues that the chain of justifying reasons must end in a reason that is not itself justified by anything further, like a First Cause that is not caused by anything outside itself. Some foundationalists think that foundational beliefs are self-justifying, whereas others think that they are not in need of justification, or that they are justified by something other than a belief, such as an experience, which is not in need of justification. (Compare this to the dispute between Plato, who thought the First Mover is self-caused, and Aristotle, who thought the First Mover is uncaused in the sense of not needing a cause.)

Many philosophers since Descartes have aimed to set our knowledge on a foundation in beliefs that are certain, thinking that by doing so, our knowledge would have the firmest possible foundation. The idea seems to be that justification weakens as it is passed along the chain of reasons, or in any case, it doesn't get any stronger. The more justified our foundational beliefs are, the better will be our justification for the beliefs that are based upon them. What could be more justified than a belief that is certain?

It depends, of course, on what you mean by "certain." People can feel certain of all sorts of things. I know a person who is certain that airplane crashes come in threes. Ann is certain that her children are smarter than Carrie's, and Carrie is certain that hers are smarter than Ann's. Some people feel certain that the theory of evolution is false and others feel certain that it is true, and so on. If certainty is just a feeling, it is not going to be a firm foundation for our knowledge because people can feel certain but be mistaken. And even if they are not mistaken, the feeling does not guarantee it. In contrast, the kind of certainty Descartes aimed for is not just a feeling. It is a state in which your feeling of being right cannot be wrong. You cannot doubt your belief, not just because of something peculiar in your psychology, but because doubt does not make sense in that case.

The ideal of certainty as the property we should aim for in our foundational (basic) beliefs has been under attack for some time now. I do not think anybody objects to the idea that certainty would be a worthy goal if it were attainable, and most philosophers probably also agree that it is attainable for a restricted class of beliefs, such as beliefs about some of our present conscious states, but unfortunately, it is difficult to see how these beliefs can be sufficient to be the ultimate justification of very many of our other beliefs. But notice that if you think the regress argument shows that the chain of justifying reasons must end, there is nothing in *that* argument that requires that the chain ends in something certain.

Let's return to the options given above. Chisholm argues that the regress ends in statements that are *self-justifying*, where a belief is self-justifying for a person just in case the person's justification for thinking he knows it to be true is simply the fact that it is true. To give the evidence for the statement believed is just to repeat it.[8] So if asked for your justification for believing that Socrates drank hemlock, you would probably refer to what you read or were taught about Socrates, but if you were asked for your justification for believing *that you believe* that Socrates drank hemlock, you would simply say, "I *do* believe Socrates drank hemlock." The fact that you have a belief justifies you in believing that you believe it. The fact that you have mental states such as hoping, wondering, and doubting justifies you in believing that you have those states. Chisholm thinks that an important class of self-justifying beliefs are beliefs about *appearances*—the way things seem to you (p. 275ff). For example, your justification for thinking that something looks white is just that it looks white. Your justification for believing something tastes sweet is that it tastes sweet. I will leave it to the reader to consider how wide the range of self-justifying beliefs is, and how wide the range of beliefs that are justified on their basis can be.[9]

Are there basic beliefs that are not self-justifying, but are justified by something other than beliefs? Alvin Plantinga argues that there must be. Suppose I have a clear memory of drinking a cup of coffee this morning. My belief expressed by the sentence, "I drank a cup of coffee this morning," does not justify itself, nor need it be justified by any other belief, such as the belief expressed by the sentence, "I seem to remember drinking coffee." Rather, the memory of drinking the coffee is an experience that directly justifies the belief that I drank a cup of coffee. The belief is foundational in that it is not based on any other *belief*, but it is not groundless; it does not appear out of nowhere.

---

[8] Chisholm (1964), p. 273.

[9] Chisholm (1964, p. 274) says that beliefs that justify themselves may also be described as neither justified nor unjustified. "The two modes of description are two different ways of saying the same thing."

Human beings are constituted in such a way that our sensory faculties in interaction with the world around us produce experiences that in turn justify beliefs. There are first-level beliefs, beliefs that are the first epistemic deliverances of our faculties. Other categories of belief are first level too, for instance, beliefs based on testimony. When a child is taught that Madrid is the capital of Spain, the child is justified in believing that Madrid is the capital of Spain. Although the child no doubt believes because he trusts the teacher, the child's justification for believing what he is taught is not dependent upon a more basic *belief* in the trustworthiness of the teacher. His experience of hearing the teacher's testimony in an environment of trust justifies his belief. Plantinga (1984) is well-known for using observations of this kind to defend the view that belief in God can be a properly basic belief, based on no other belief, but based on various kinds of experience, either religious or testimonial.[10]

Coherentists object that foundationalist theories cannot avoid ending the regress in something arbitrary. Of course, it may not seem to *us* that it is arbitrary, but if we are conscientious believers, we need a reason to think that whatever stops the regress has the right property, a property that makes it justified and capable of conferring justification on the beliefs that depend upon it. But what would justify us in thinking that? Some philosophers have abandoned foundationalism and have embraced what seems to be the only alternative left by the regress argument except skepticism: coherentism. Laurence BonJour and Keith Lehrer are (or were) coherentists. According to coherence theories of justification, the chain of justifying reasons eventually circles back on itself, so the chain of justification looks like a big circle like this:

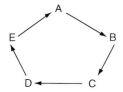

or perhaps a more complicated network like this:

---

[10] For a more developed account, see Plantinga (2000).

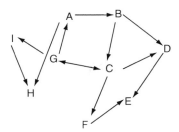

What makes the circle or network coherent is that there are no breaks in the arrows (no beliefs that are not justified by other beliefs in the network).

BonJour defends another possibility, that coherence is a property possessed by the network as a whole. An example of holistic coherence is the classic English detective novel. A particular clue may justify the detective in drawing a particular conclusion, for instance, that Colonel Mustard was in the library at 7:00, but, more importantly, the belief that Colonel Mustard was in the library at 7:00 is justified by its part in a story in which all the pieces "fit." What makes each belief in the network justified is not simply its connection to particular pieces of evidence, but the fact that all the pieces together have the property we call coherence. The whole story "makes sense," as we say. Making sense is not a property of any individual belief, but is a property of the entire set of beliefs. According to this version of the coherence theory, the regress problem is avoided by abandoning the view that justification is linear in favor of the view that it is holistic.

But is coherence sufficient for justification? It is well-known that intelligent paranoids can come up with very coherent stories to explain their paranoid view of the world. No matter what evidence you give them, they can make it fit their paranoid picture. A coherent body of beliefs may therefore have nothing to do with the way the world really is. But this objection does not necessarily make foundationalism look better because self-justifying beliefs may not have anything to do with the way the world really is either. That is because examples typically given of self-justifying beliefs are about the contents of one's own mind or what appears to be such and such, and such beliefs may have nothing to do with the world outside our minds. But the foundationalist can agree, and then go on to reiterate that beliefs justified by their justified connections to self-justifying beliefs are justified. Coherentists can do the same thing. They can agree that a coherent set of beliefs is no guarantee of truth, but if the issue is justification, coherence is the best we can get, and it is good enough. The regress argument, after all, is not about guarantees, but about the justification needed for knowledge.

Is there any other option? Peter Klein argues that the coherentist is right that foundationalism makes justification rest on something arbitrary, and the foundationalist is right that coherentism makes our justification circular, and both are unacceptable. Klein (1999) argues for what he calls **infinitism**, the theory that a justified belief is justified by an infinite sequence of reasons. This is not a skeptical consequence, says Klein, because an infinite sequence of reasons *does* justify each of our justified beliefs. Klein is not suggesting that we can keep an infinite set of reasons in our heads or access all of them on demand, but he says that that is not necessary.

Foundationalists and coherentists agree that a justifying reason can support a belief when the believer is not aware of it. Consider testimony. Suppose I am justified in believing that some event happened in ancient China due to a long chain of testimony leading back to somebody's observation two thousand years ago. I am not aware of very much of that chain and never was, but that does not prevent me from being justified in my belief. Suppose now that the chain is not only very long, it is infinitely long. We have already seen that there are objections to the possibility of an infinitely long chain that parallel the First Cause Argument for theism, but that possibility cannot be discounted out of hand, as traditional proponents of the regress argument have done.

If we accept the first three premises of the regress argument, it does look like our options are limited to foundationalism, coherentism, infinitism, or skepticism. We could, of course, reject one of the premises. There are a number of ways we might do that, some of which we will discuss later in this chapter.

III. THE SECOND STAGE OF THE SKEPTICAL ATTACK: DESCARTES'S EVIL GENIUS AND THE IRRELEVANCE OF EVIDENCE

A. The Evil Genius

Skepticism fell out of favor for many hundreds of years. In the fifth century Augustine wrote against the skeptics of antiquity, but it was not until approximately the sixteenth century in the work of Montaigne that skepticism regained prominence among philosophers. Montaigne was familiar with Pyrrhonian skepticism and discussed it in essays that were highly popular among the intellectuals of his time.[11] Descartes knew Montaigne's work, but his form of skepticism is quite different. The revolution in science that replaced the Ptolemaic view of the solar system made a profound impact on Descartes. In the sixteenth century Copernicus had proposed that the planets must revolve around the sun, based on mathematical evidence, but it was not until 1609 that the Copernican heliocentric view of the solar system was proven by the evidence of Galileo's telescope. Even though the evidence for the Ptolemaic viewpoint had seemed to be overwhelming, it was nonetheless proven false. This led Descartes to think that much of what passes for scientific knowledge is based on a flimsy foundation, the foundation of sensory perception. Since so many of our beliefs are based on sense experience, if that foundation falls apart, so do most of our beliefs. The conscientious believer should take this as a cautionary warning: Even when the evidence in support of some belief is apparently strong, it might be false.

But Descartes would not be so famous if all he did was to point out that sense experience is insufficient to support scientific theories. In Descartes's first *Meditation*, he proposes to doubt any belief that is not certain, not because he proposes to henceforth believe only what is certain, but because he thinks that if he can find something that *is* certain, he will have found something that can serve as a firm foundation for his beliefs. His famous test for certainty and doubt is the following:

> If hypothesis H is possible, and if belief B is false on H, then B is not certain and should be doubted. If there is no H which is such that H is possible and B is false on H, then B is certain.

Descartes then proposes two hypotheses that he thinks will permit him to doubt large numbers of his beliefs at once, including beliefs based on sense experience and most other categories of belief, such as beliefs in mathematics and arguably some (but not all) of the principles of reason.

In the Dream hypothesis, Descartes argues that since there are no definitive signs to distinguish waking and dreaming, he might be dreaming even now. He then argues roughly as follows:

---

[11] See Montaigne (1958), especially the section "Apology for Raymond Sebond," subsection "Man Has No Knowledge."

(i) It is possible that I am dreaming.

(ii) If I am dreaming then many of my beliefs would be false.

Therefore,

(iii) It is possible that those beliefs are false. Those beliefs are not certain and I should doubt them.

Descartes then observes that some things cannot be doubted even in dreams. We can dream of animals that do not exist, but even if there are no such animals, there at least have to be the colors and shapes that are the fundamental building blocks of our more complex ideas of animals. Furthermore, in a dream I can follow a line of argument (up to a point) and do simple arithmetic. My dream calculator may be unreliable, but I can add 3 and 5 just as well in a dream as in waking life.[12]

This leads Descartes to turn to a hypothesis that permits him even more extensive doubt, his **Evil Genius hypothesis**. The reasoning of this hypothesis parallels the reasoning above: It is possible there is an Evil Genius (EG), a being powerful enough to tamper with my mind, giving me the illusion of living my life even though there is no physical world and possibly never has been such a world or any other being besides myself and the EG. If there were an EG, then not only would my sensory beliefs be false, but I could be fooled about many other categories of belief, including beliefs based on simple arithmetic. It follows that all these beliefs might be false. They are not certain and should be doubted.

The EG hypothesis is the most radical test Descartes can think of. We are all familiar with contemporary versions of this hypothesis in science fiction stories in which a person lives for an extended time with an implant in his brain that gives him the illusion of living a life he is not living at all. *The Matrix* movies are versions of Descartes's hypothesis. It might seem extreme to subject our beliefs to the test, "Would this belief be true even if I were living in the Matrix?," but the advantage of using such a radical hypothesis is that *if* a belief can pass the test, we can justifiably conclude that it is certain and indubitable, assuming that there is no other hypothesis we have not thought of that is also possible and which is such that on that hypothesis the belief is false. Descartes thought that some beliefs do past the test and therefore ought to be the foundation of our entire system of beliefs.

---

[12] Descartes (1984), vol. II, p. 14.

Once we see the optimistic side of Descartes, his rigorous method of doubt does not look so ominous, but the historical verdict on Descartes is that his attempt to construct a firm foundation for all ordinary beliefs is unsuccessful. Many philosophers think that if we accept his method of doubt, we end up believing very little. For that reason, Descartes has been frequently accused of having unreasonably stringent requirements for knowledge, requiring a test for certainty that goes well beyond anything we think a conscientious believer ought to have, and going well beyond the conditions necessary for knowledge.

But it is not at all clear that Descartes is guilty of using excessively stringent requirements for knowledge or conscientious belief in his skeptical hypotheses. To see why not, let's look at the EG hypothesis as a test for knowledge. Descartes is claiming the following:

> (S) I do not know there is a table here unless I know there is
> no EG fooling me.

Does (S) require more than we usually require for knowledge? We often say that we do not know something unless we can tell the difference between a situation in which it is true and a situation in which it is false.[13] We use this test all the time. For example, suppose you are looking at an acquaintance and you believe it is Tom. But Tom has a twin brother Tim who looks enough like Tom that if you had been looking at Tim, you would have thought you were seeing Tom. Do you know it is Tom? A jury in a murder trial in which you are the witness and Tom is the defendant would probably say you do not know. If you cannot distinguish Tom from Tim, you do not know that the man you saw was Tom. The principle the jury would use in Tom's trial might be something like this:

> (T) You do not know you saw Tom unless you know the
> man you saw is not Tim.

And this principle seems to make it reasonable for us to use the parallel principle (S).

But maybe the jury in Tom's trial would only adopt (T) if Tim were in the vicinity and the person you saw could easily have been Tim. What if, unknown to you, Tim was on an Arctic expedition at the time? It

---

[13] Even Plato uses this test in an exchange in the *Theaetetus* when Socrates proposes to Theaetetus that knowledge requires "being able to tell some mark by which the object you are asked about differs from all other things" (208c).

seems to me that the jury would conclude that you probably saw Tom, although it is doubtful that they would conclude that you *knew* you saw Tom. Even though they might accept your testimony as evidence that you saw Tom, I see no reason to think they would abandon (T).

But what if Tom's lawyer argued that you did not know you saw Tom because you would not have been able to distinguish Tom from a twin brother who does not exist but might have existed? Surely the jury would reject (T) if "Tim" is just the name of a hypothetical twin brother Tom might have had. Similarly, those who accuse Descartes of using unreasonably stringent criteria for knowledge might say that since there is no EG and the existence of an EG scenario is no more than a bare possibility, (S) is false for the same reason (T) is false when Tom has no twin brother and the existence of a twin is merely possible.

But unfortunately, the cases are not analogous. In the Tom case, there are ways of finding out whether Tom has a twin brother and his probable whereabouts independent of what you, the witness, saw and knew. This background information can be taken into account in evaluating the evidence that you knew you saw Tom. But in the EG hypothesis, the background evidence itself is affected by the EG hypothesis. The EG would presumably be clever enough to make his existence seem highly improbable even if he existed. The EG scenario predicts that the situation would *seem* analogous to seeing Tom when he has no twin brother even though the situation would actually be analogous to seeing Tom when he *does* have an identical twin brother who was around at the time.

To make the Tom case closer to the EG case, we would have to imagine that there is no way to tell whether Tom has a twin brother, since all the witnesses would swear there is no twin brother even if there were. Even then the case is not analogous to the EG case because at least we have background evidence of the probability that any person taken at random has an identical twin brother, but we have no evidence at all of the probability that there is an EG. Of course it seems to us highly improbable that there is an EG, but it would seem that way in any case. This makes it very difficult to evaluate the claim that the standards for (S) are more stringent than ordinary standards for knowing. We don't seem to have parallel cases with which to compare it.

Perhaps the main reason we might think that (S) is true is that we are inclined to accept the following **Principle of Epistemic Closure**:

If S knows that *p* entails *q*, then if S knows *p*, S knows *q*, which is equivalent to:

> If S knows that p entails q, then if S does not know q, then S does not know p.

This leads us to a variation of the skeptical argument:

The Evil Genius Closure Argument

(1) If I know that p entails *not q*, then if I don't know *not q*, I don't know p. (Principle of Epistemic Closure)

(2) I know that *There is a table in front of me* entails *There is no EG fooling me.*

(3) I do not know *There is no EG fooling me.*

Therefore,

(4) I do not know *There is a table in front of me.*

This form of skepticism may be more threatening than the regress argument because it seems to make all our evidence irrelevant. Even if the problem of the regress of evidence can be solved and our beliefs can be justified by evidence, the EG hypothesis raises doubts about the connection between evidence and truth. No matter how strong the evidence for a belief is, if it would be false under the hypothesis of an EG, we do not know it. To return to the analogy with Tom and Tim, no matter how strong my evidence is that I am seeing Tom, if I cannot rule out the possibility that he is Tim, I don't know that I see Tom.

In section II we looked at foundationalism and coherentism as ways to avoid the infinite regress problem. Can they be used to avoid Cartesian skepticism as well? Descartes presupposed foundationalism in his method of doubt, arguing that if a foundational belief is dubitable, so are the beliefs based upon it, and he argued that if any beliefs survive the test of the skeptical hypotheses, those beliefs are certain and can serve as the foundation of a justified system of beliefs. As we all know, there is a belief that survives the test, Descartes's famous *"Cogito, ergo sum"* ("I think, therefore, I am"), and Descartes courageously argued that the *cogito* (along with a few logical or metaphysical principles) is sufficient to be the basis of a comprehensive system of beliefs, including most of what we ordinarily believe, such as the existence of an external physical world. Unfortunately, subsequent philosophers have thought that what survives the skeptical hypothesis is not sufficient to hold up the edifice of a system of beliefs that includes ordinary beliefs about the existence of a physical world and other persons. If they are right, the skeptic is still the winner. Even though there are some beliefs that survive the skeptical attack, most do not. Foundationalism still has adherents, but its pretensions to answer the challenge of Cartesian skepticism have withered.[14]

Coherentism about justification would not avoid EG skepticism since the latter is not about justification, but about the connection between justification (or evidence) and truth. Suppose, however, that coherentism about justification is combined with coherentism about truth. That is, suppose that what makes a belief true is just that it coheres with one's other beliefs. Truth is a property beliefs have when they are members of a coherent belief set. I find coherentism about truth implausible, but it has the advantage of avoiding both forms of skepticism we have considered. Perhaps that will give some readers a motive for taking it seriously.

B. Denial of Epistemic Closure

We now turn to three contemporary responses to Cartesian skepticism. First, let's look at the logical structure of the Evil Genius Closure argument. The form of the argument is simple; (2)–(4) is a standard *modus tollens* argument form. But suppose we turn the argument around, as G. E. Moore did by arguing as follows:

G. E. Moore's Antiskeptical Argument

(1') If I know that p entails *not q*, then if I know p, I know *not q*. (equivalent to Closure principle (1) above)

(2') I know that *There is a table in front of me* entails *There is no EG fooling me*. (same as (2) above)

(3') I know *there is a table in front of me*.

Therefore,

(4') I know *there is no EG fooling me*.[15]

---

[14] Timothy McGrew (1995) and Richard Fumerton (2001) use Cartesian-style approaches to skepticism and are exceptions to my claim above.

[15] See Moore (1959), pp. 223–26.

This argument, like the EG closure argument, assumes the closure principle, except that G. E. Moore's argument uses *modus ponens,* whereas the skeptical argument uses *modus tollens.* Moore's objectors point out that the argument above does not count as *evidence* that I know there is no EG, but Moore's supporters can say that the EG closure argument does not count as evidence that I don't know there is a table in front of me. One side says we should argue from (3) to (4), while the other side says we should argue from (3') to (4'). The two sides seem to be at an impasse. A more promising response to skepticism, argues Fred Dretske (1970), is the denial of (1).

Dretske argues that there are lots of counterexamples to the principle of epistemic closure. The closest cases to the one used by the skeptic are contrast cases such as the following. Suppose you go to the zoo and you see animals that look just like zebras in a cage clearly marked "zebras." Presumably, you know they are zebras. You also know that if they are zebras they are not mules in disguise. But, Dretske argues, you do not know they are not mules in disguise. That is because the evidence that something is a zebra differs from the evidence that something is not a mule in disguise. Evidence that something is a zebra includes the fact that the animals look and behave like zebras, are identified as zebras by the zoo staff, and are in a cage marked "zebras." Evidence that something is not a mule in disguise is different. It presumably would include a very close examination of the animals and the way they have been previously handled, as well as evidence of the zoo staff's motives. You can easily have evidence of the former sort but not the latter.

Similarly, evidence that this is a table is just that it looks like a table, holds your cup when you set it down, and is called a "table" by others, whereas evidence that you are not being fooled by an EG is evidence you simply do not have and never will have. How could you ever be in a position to determine whether there is an Evil Genius in existence or that you are living in the Matrix? Dretske's answer to the skeptical argument, then, is that the first premise is false. You know there is a table in front of you even though you do not know there is no EG. So both (3) and (3') are true. Ordinary knowledge claims are immune to the skeptical hypothesis.

Readers may find it fun to think about the closure principle and possible counterexamples. Which is more convincing—the examples, or the closure principle? In thinking through these cases there is always the problem that we might not be sure of our own intellectual honesty. If we want a successful response to the skeptical argument badly enough, we might reject principles we would not otherwise reject, such as closure. On the other hand, the closure principle gets its believability from examples. It is not self-evident and it is not demonstrable. Likewise, we might feel sure of both closure and the rejection of the skeptical argument, in which case we might be attracted to G. E. Moore's argument. But is that argument anything more than a statement of faith?

C. Reliabilism

Some philosophers think that the best, and perhaps only response to the skeptic is to start over again and change the terms of the debate about whether knowledge is possible. Reliabilism is one theory that does that. The impetus for reliabilism was an early paper by W. V. Quine called "Epistemology Naturalized" (Quine, 1969), in which Quine argued that knowledge is a natural phenomenon and should be investigated empirically the way we investigate other processes in nature. In Chapter One we saw that in most of the ancient and medieval periods knowledge was treated as the outgrowth of the study of human nature and the nature of the world, so epistemology was continuous with metaphysics. Contemporary naturalized epistemologists see it as continuous with science. The approach is not identical, but the motive is much the same. In both cases epistemology is treated as less basic than some other field, a field that describes the most general features of the world.

When reliabilists treat knowledge as a natural phenomenon, they shift the focus of epistemological questions from the point of view of the subject to the point of view of an observer of the subject. This brings up the important distinction between **internalism** and **externalism** in epistemology. Assume that knowledge is true belief + x. Internalists maintain, roughly, that x must be something accessible to the mind of the knower, whereas externalists deny that. The two skeptical arguments we have studied are formulated from an internalist perspective because it is assumed that in order to know p, the knower must have reasons or evidence for her belief that p. Granted, the idea of reasons for a belief is vague, but it would be usual to interpret it in a way that requires that the reasons justifying a belief be accessible to the subject herself. Indeed, the regress argument assumes that the subject bases her belief upon those reasons.

The externalist, in contrast, looks for features of the subject's belief state or process of coming to believe that can be attributed to the subject from outside her perspective. Of course, some of these features may be accessible to her, but some may not. If knowledge is a natural phenomenon investigated by a science of knowledge, there is no more reason to expect the features of epistemic states that make them states of knowing to be accessible to the subject than there is to expect the features of an animal that make it a kangaroo to be accessible to the kangaroo. Or to get a parallel that is closer to the case of knowing, consider memory. Remembering is a natural conscious phenomenon, but we do not expect that a person can tell from the inside that her putative memory of what happened is an actual memory of what happened. That is, the conditions that distinguish a state of actual memory from mistaken memory are not conditions that the subject herself can determine. Similarly, the conditions that distinguish a state of actually knowing from a state that is not knowing but seems to be knowing to the subject, may not be conditions that the subject can determine.

Now you might reply, "Well, of course not, but that's just because knowing entails truth, and we don't think that the subject can tell from the inside that her belief is true. But she *can* tell if her belief has the additional component of knowledge other than truth." But why think that? There are plenty of features of our mental states that we are unable to access. Maybe the feature of knowing that distinguishes it from mere true believing is one of them. Can you always tell that you are virtuously motivated, or thinking clearly, or free of self-deception? If not, maybe you can't always tell when you have the mysterious feature that converts true belief into knowledge.

In Chapter Five we will look at a problem with reliabilism that I consider serious. In this chapter we are concerned with the way that reliabilism can be used as a way out of skepticism. There are many forms of reliabilism, but according to the simplest and most straightforward version, what makes a true belief an instance of knowledge is that it was formed by a reliable process for obtaining the truth. Reliable processes include perception and memory, the reliability of which need not be cognitively accessible to the believer, and so reliabilism is a form of externalism. Alvin Goldman (1979) proposed an early version of reliabilism. Subsequent versions are somewhat more complicated, focusing on reliable faculties (Sosa, 1994, 1997) or reliable agents (Greco, 1999). Most reliabilists think that an advantage of reliabilism is that its standards are generous, allowing for knowledge among children and unsophisticated adults. The avoidance of skepticism is taken to be one of its strengths.

How would reliabilism escape skepticism? Notice first that it seems to avoid the regress problem because the reliabilist denies that knowledge requires a propositional justification that in turn must have a propositional justification. All you need for knowledge is to be hooked up to the world in the right way. So suppose you believe you see a bright red tulip and you are, in fact, looking at a red tulip, and the processes that lead you to that belief are features of yourself and your environment that generally lead the subject to true beliefs. You and your environment are reliably attuned, and in the natural course of events, you get a true belief. The reliabilist will say that that is all it takes for knowledge. Furthermore, the reliabilist denies that you need to know or believe anything about Evil Geniuses in order to know that you are looking at a red tulip. A process that reliably leads to the belief that there is no Evil Genius might not be the same as the process that reliably leads to the belief that there is a red tulip in front of you. Your belief that you see a red tulip can be reliably formed and constitute knowledge, if true, even if you have no answer to Descartes or other skeptical assaults on your belief.

Does that mean that the reliabilist must deny the closure principle? Typically reliabilists deny closure, but whether they must, or even can do so is not clear. The reliabilist acknowledges that various forms of inference are reliable processes for extending our knowledge. Concluding that q from the conjunction of p and $p \rightarrow q$ is one of the most highly reliable of all belief-forming processes. So if I know p and I know that p entails q, surely I know that q. It seems, then, that the reliabilist is committed to the closure principle. If the reliabilist accepts closure, he or she can still escape the Evil Genius Closure argument by way of G. E. Moore's argument, and perhaps reliabilism with closure is a reason to accept Moore's (3'), but in that case the work of rejecting the skeptical closure argument comes from Moore's strategy, not reliabilism. On the other hand, if the reliabilist rejects closure, the work of rejecting the skeptical closure argument comes from the rejection of the closure principle, not reliabilism. Either way, the reliabilist's way out of the skeptical argument above does not come from reliabilism *per se*.

Suppose that reliabilism succeeds as a theory of knowledge according to which we have knowledge without an answer to the skeptical hypothesis and without needing to worry about the infinite regress. Does that mean we have avoided skepticism? Maybe not, for reliabilism can be used as an answer to skepticism only if (a) we are, in fact, reliably hooked up to the world, (b) reliabilism is the correct theory of knowledge, and (c) we know (a) and (b). But even if (a) and (b) are true and we know (a), do we know (b) according to the theory? It follows from reliabilism that we know the theory is true provided that (i) the theory is true, and (ii) our belief that the theory is true is produced by a process that is reliably hooked up to the world. If the process that produced the theory of reliabilism is a reliable process, then if the theory is true, we know that it is. But even though it is plausible that we have reliable processes for producing many ordinary beliefs, how plausible is it that an epistemological theory is produced by a reliable process? When philosophers propose new theories, do they use processes of reasoning and reflection that generally produce true beliefs and this is just one more? That hardly explains what is going on in the case of coming to believe a philosophical theory, and it is particularly problematic when one has invented the theory oneself.

The deeper reason why reliabilism does not seem to give a convincing answer to the skeptic is that reliabilism asks us to move to an externalist theory of knowledge in order to answer a problem that arises from an internalist perspective. At the end of Chapter One I suggested that the reason skepticism has gotten so much attention from philosophers is that we *care* that the world is more or less the way we think it is, and we would feel cheated if we were systematically misled about reality by living in a skeptical scenario. We believe we are not living in a skeptical scenario and it is very important to us that that belief is true. Since caring imposes a demand on us to be conscientious in that belief, the demand is not met if we have reasons to think that the belief is not conscientious, or at least, not as conscientious as it should be, given the level of importance the belief has to us. The fact that there is a theory of knowledge according to which our ordinary beliefs are cases of knowledge does not address the issue of conscientiousness in the belief that we are not living in a skeptical scenario.

A related objection applies to Dretske's denial of the Closure Principle. Dretske seems to think that skepticism has been answered as long as I know and have good reason to believe that there is a table in front of me, even though he agrees with the skeptic that I do not know or have good reason to believe that I am not living in a skeptical scenario. But if I *care* that I am not living in a skeptical scenario, then I put a demand on myself to be conscientious in my belief that I am not so living, and Dretske's denial of Closure does not permit me to do that.

D. Contextualism

Contextualism is a more recent response to skepticism than reliabilism and the denial of the Closure Principle, and it is doubtful that it would have been developed had it been thought that either of the other two ways out of skepticism were fully satisfactory. The denial of closure is a particularly bitter pill to swallow, but Dretske's discussion of contrast cases led David Lewis (1996) to a less extreme solution.

Recall Dretske's example of knowing that the animals in the cage are zebras. Dretske argued that you know they are zebras even though you have not eliminated every alternative to their being zebras, such as their being mules in disguise. You know they are zebras because you have the evidence relevant to being zebras, but you do not know they are not mules in disguise since that requires different evidence, evidence you do not have.

Now Lewis says that he thinks Dretske got the phenomenon right but gave the wrong diagnosis (p. 564). In order to know *p*, you must eliminate alternatives to *p*, but *only those relevant to a given context.* In ordinary circumstances, if you visit the zoo and see a cage marked "zebras" containing animals that look just like zebras and are called "zebras" by the staff, then you know they are zebras. There are no other *relevant* possibilities that you have not eliminated. However, we can imagine a situation in which the possibility that the animals in the zebra cage are mules in disguise is relevant. Perhaps there is evidence that the zebras died and the zoo keeper has a motive to cover it up. Or perhaps there is no such evidence, but that possibility is raised by a participant in the discussion. Lewis says that in that case, the parties to the discussion do not know the animals in the cage are zebras because the possibility that they are disguised mules is relevant and has not been eliminated. This move permits Lewis to retain the Closure principle within a given context, while simultaneously explaining why it is not necessary to eliminate every alternative to *p* in order to know *p*.

Lewis defines knowledge as follows:

> S knows that *p* if and only if *p* holds in every possibility left uneliminated by S's evidence (except for those possibilities that we are properly ignoring). (p. 561)

Lewis proposes the following rules to determine what we may and may not properly ignore in the context of a discussion of whether some subject has knowledge.

Rule of Actuality. We may not ignore the truth. If zoo personnel have a motive to paint mules to look like zebras, we may not safely ignore it. If Tom has a twin brother who looks just like him, we may not ignore it. Notice that this is an externalist rule. Maybe we are not aware of Tom's twin brother, or we are not aware of the zoo staff's motives, but we may not ignore it even though we are unaware of it. Our ignorance of what we cannot properly ignore can take away knowledge.

Rule of Belief. Something the subject believes is not properly ignored whether or not he is right to believe it. If the subject believes that Tom has a twin, he may not ignore it even if Tom does not have a twin. If I believe the zoo personnel have a motive to paint mules to look like zebras, I may not properly ignore it even if the zoo personnel have no such motive. What I believe affects what I know even if what I believe is false.

Rule of Resemblance. We may not ignore a possibility that is relevantly similar to one we are not ignoring. Lewis says he does not know how to ignore the Evil Genius hypothesis since that possibility does resemble some possibilities we are not ignoring. As I said above in discussing the similarity of the possibility of an EG and the possibility that Tom has a twin, it is hard to say whether the skeptical scenario really is similar to possibilities we do not ignore, but I will let the reader decide on that issue.

Rule of Reliability. We are entitled to assume that our faculties are functioning reliably (or properly). This rule is defeasible, of course. The idea is that we may assume our faculties are functioning properly until we have reason to think that they are not. So we are entitled to place implicit trust in our belief-forming faculties.

Rule of Conservatism. We may safely ignore what most of the people around us ignore. If most of the people around us ignore the possibility that the zebras are mules in disguise, we may also. If most of the people around us ignore the EG hypothesis, we may also.

Rule of Attention. We are not properly ignoring a possibility that is brought to our attention. We cannot be properly ignoring something if we are not ignoring it. So once the possibility that the zebras are mules in disguise is brought up, we are no longer properly ignoring it. Once the EG possibility is brought up, we can no longer be properly ignoring it. That means that what we know in the context of an epistemology discussion is more restricted than what we know in ordinary discussions outside the classroom. That is because more alternatives to what we think we know are brought up in epistemology discussions than in ordinary life. That is why knowledge is elusive, according to Lewis. If you mention a possibility you are not ignoring it, and if you are not ignoring it you are not properly ignoring it. So once you even think of an Evil Genius, that takes away your knowledge. Curiously, we would have known more if we had been less imaginative. That is why the definition of knowledge Lewis proposes has an important qualifier. What he actually says is this:

> S knows that p if and only if p holds in every possibility left unelimated by S's evidence—Psst, except for those possibilities that *we* are properly ignoring. (p. 561)

What follows "psst" is meant to be something whispered behind the hand, alerting the participants in the discussion to be careful what alternatives they think about!

Notice that the conditions for whether S knows p include a reference to alternatives "we" may properly ignore. By "we" Lewis means the speaker and hearer discussing whether S has knowledge, so Lewis's theory is what is commonly called **attributor-based contextualism**. That is, the context pertinent to whether a subject has knowledge is determined by the context of those discussing whether S knows, not S's context.

There are other forms of contextualism that are **subject-based**. In this form of contextualism, the context is determined by the subject. For example, suppose we are discussing whether Jim knows that the bank closes on Friday at 5:00.[16] Jim seems to remember that he has previously been to the bank at 4:45 on a Friday, so we might say that he has good reason to believe it closes at 5:00, so if it is true that it closes at 5:00, Jim knows that it does. But now suppose that Jim considers it imperative that he get to the bank before closing on Friday. Once we find out the gravity of his need, we might say that on second thought, Jim does not know that the bank is open until 5:00. According to this version of contextualism, then, the context relevant to whether Jim knows the time the bank closes is given by Jim's concerns, not ours. Subject-based contextualism has a curious implication, however. There can be two people, Jim and Mary, who have exactly the same reasons for thinking the bank closes at 5:00, but if it is more

---

[16] See DeRose (1995).

important to Jim that he get to the bank before closing than it is to Mary, Mary knows the bank closes at 5:00 and Jim does not.

How does contextualism answer the two skeptical problems we have considered in this chapter? According to Lewis's version of contextualism, the regress of justifying reasons for a belief ends in a belief that need not be justified in the context because all parties agree to it. We simply end our sequence of justification when we get to something for which all relevant alternatives have been eliminated. Presumably, in most contexts of discussion that happens rather quickly, but of course, there is no guarantee that it happens quickly in all contexts. EG skepticism is not relevant to most contexts of discussion, but since it clearly *is* relevant in philosophy discussions, Lewis's form of contextualism does not avoid the EG closure argument for people reading this book while they are reading or thinking about it. However, once you stop reading and forget about the EG, you will properly attribute much more knowledge to yourself and others than you did while studying epistemology!

Subject-based contextualism answers skepticism in a different way. It makes the things the subject cares about relevant to what she knows. Just as Jim does not know the bank closes at 5:00 based on ordinary memory if it is highly important to him to get there before closing, so too, Jim does not know most of the ordinary things he thinks he knows if it is highly important to him that there is no Evil Genius. Standards are lower the less you care, higher as your caring increases, so according to this version of contextualism, the way to avoid EG skepticism is not to care.

It is hard to see how contextualism helps the conscientious believer. You are the same person when you study epistemology or watch *The Matrix* as you are when you forget about skepticism and do something else. Once you stop thinking about skepticism it may slip into the back of your mind, but once you have been exposed to it, it will always be there, and you can forget it only if you engage in some rather serious self-deception. So Lewis's approach allows you to conscientiously maintain ordinary beliefs only if you con yourself into ignoring skeptical possibilities. On the DeRose approach you can conscientiously maintain your beliefs only if you con yourself into not caring. Neither is a very convincing response to skepticism for conscientious belief even if it is an answer to skepticism about knowledge.

In this chapter we have looked at how the possibility of an Evil Genius threatens skepticism via the closure argument of section

III.A. But arguably, the EG scenario simply calls attention to the possibility of a rift between mind and reality that is already latent in a common view of the relation between mind and world. The source of skepticism we will discuss in the next chapter is also Cartesian, but it does not require that we take the possibility of an EG seriously. In my opinion, the form of skepticism we will discuss next is the hardest of all.

FURTHER READING

For an array of historical texts on different forms of skepticism and other skeptical topics, see Charles Landesman and Robin Meeks (eds.), *Philosophical Skepticism* (Oxford: Blackwell Publishers, 2003). More advanced students should look at Keith DeRose and Ted Warfield (eds.), *Skepticism: A Contemporary Reader* (Oxford: Oxford University Press, 1999), which includes several of the approaches to skepticism discussed in this chapter, including reliabilism, contextualism, and the denial of closure. A fascinating survey and critique of foundationalism, coherentism, internalism, and reliabilism/externalism can be found in Alvin Plantinga's *Warrant: The Current Debate* (Oxford: Oxford University Press, 1993). Hilary Kornblith's anthology, *Epistemology: Internalism and Externalism* (Oxford: Blackwell, 2001) is a collection of essays by several leading epistemologists regarding the internalism/externalism debate. A truly unique book, Ernest Sosa and Laurence BonJour's *Epistemic Justification: Internalism vs. Externalism, Foundations vs. Virtues* (Oxford: Blackwell Publishing, 2003) presents a debate in which BonJour develops a detailed account and defense of internalist foundationalism, while Sosa does the same for externalist views of virtues.

3

Mind and World: Metaphysical and Semantic Responses to Skepticism

I. THE THIRD STAGE OF THE SKEPTICAL ATTACK: THE ABSOLUTE CONCEPTION OF REALITY

In this chapter we will look at a completely different point of entry into skepticism. The problem posed in Chapter Two was that skepticism seems to be the outcome of certain very compelling arguments. Although the arguments are forceful, once the argumentative structure is displayed, we may be able to identify ways to escape the conclusion. In contrast, the skeptical threat we will discuss in this chapter does not arise from an argument. Rather, a very inviting conception of the relation between the subject and the object of knowledge makes the danger of skepticism imminent. It appears that all we have to do is to think carefully about what knowledge is to see that it may be beyond our powers to get it.

As noted in Chapter One, one of the few points of agreement among philosophers on the nature of knowledge is that it is a relation between a conscious subject and an object, where the object is some part of reality. The subject seeks to correctly grasp the part of reality at which it is directed. The quest for knowledge, then, is a quest for what the world is really like, not what it appears to be. A more controversial way to put it is that the reality we seek to know is reality untampered by our minds, "what there is anyway," in the words of Bernard Williams (1978, p. 64). Yet another way to express the same idea is that it is a conception of the world as it would be underwritten by God. Williams calls this the **absolute conception of reality**.

Specifically, Williams proposes that the absolute conception of reality (ACR) arises from two assumptions about knowledge:

(1) If knowledge is possible, it has to be possible to form a coherent conception of its object.[1]

(2) The object of knowledge is something independent of that knowledge itself, and, indeed, independent of . . . any thought or experience.[2] (Ibid)

A conception that satisfies (1) and (2) is what Williams means by the ACR. Notice that successfully satisfying both requirements does not guarantee knowledge, but we are in trouble if we cannot do both. That is, we would know that we have failed to get knowledge if we cannot form a coherent conception of a mind-independent reality.

But skeptical danger lurks in the idea of a mind-independent reality because it includes the idea of a gap between the mind and the reality grasped by the mind. Gaps are often bridgeable, but on what basis can we trust that our minds are capable of constructing a conception of something that, by hypothesis, has nothing to do with the mind? The problem is not that we have an argument that it is impossible, but that we need an argument that it is possible and we have no such argument. In fact, it is hard to see how it is even possible to have an argument that it is possible to bridge the gap. The ACR is therefore "a standing invitation to skepticism" (Williams, p. 64).

A related difficulty arises from the conception of the mind as *representing* reality. Representation need not mean mirroring or

---

[1] I don't think Williams's point (1) can apply to negative knowledge. I can know that a square circle does not exist precisely because I *can't* form a coherent conception of it.

[2] Williams is not denying that there is knowledge of one's own mental states, but that is a special case.

copying, but whatever representation is, it is a relation between two distinct, and, indeed, different things—the thing doing the representing and the thing represented. As long as that relation can systematically fail, the grounds for skepticism are already there.

Who first thought of the absolute conception of reality? Williams thinks Descartes gets the credit, but the two constraints on the possibility of knowledge identified by Williams do not seem to me to require an especially Cartesian method or philosophical viewpoint. What undoubtedly did originate with Descartes was the association of the attempt to form the ACR with the attempt to get certainty (Williams, pp. 67, 247). This association is unfortunate because it can lead us to think that if we reject the ideal of certainty on the grounds that it is too rigorous, a standard for knowledge, we have thereby refuted the ACR.

But the ACR cannot be rejected that easily. The two constraints on knowledge identified by Williams have nothing to do with certainty or Evil Geniuses, nor do they have anything to do with infinite regresses. They are arguably nothing but a clarification of what we *mean* by knowledge, and if so, the potential for skepticism does not rest on unreasonable demands for certainty, outrageous hypotheses, or the peculiarities of the formulation of the regress argument. The potential for skepticism is inherent in the way we think of knowledge. If that is right, skepticism is going to be very hard to avoid without giving up (1) or (2). Few people give up (1), but (2) has been attacked in various ways, some of which we will survey in this chapter.

Before looking at ways to reject the ACR, let us pause to think about what is attractive and compelling about it. It seems to me that it is an important aspect of human nature to try to move outside of ourselves. We have the urge to do that with our intellects, with our senses, with our emotions, and through our actions. We try to make the universe outside our minds present to our consciousness through knowledge. Most of the time, of course, only a small part of the universe is present to us, the part that we detect through the senses, and to which we respond in our emotions and choices. We then act in order to affect the outside world; we try to make a difference to that world. Of course, we could make a difference without understanding what it is we are affecting, but we think that the world is what is there *in advance* of our sensing, knowing, and acting. In fact, we think that the world was there long before our birth or the birth of any creatures with our faculties. If we grasp or understand the world in a way that depends upon our minds, that cannot be the way the world was in advance. To be confident of emotions such as love, anger, fear, compassion, or joy, we need to get clear on exactly what is in the world that is the appropriate object of such emotions. If we do not understand the world clearly, the emotions we have toward that world may be misdirected. The same point applies to actions. Our efforts in action seem to be wasted if we do not grasp the world as it really is before trying to affect it in some way.

There are philosophers who think that getting a clear and consistent conception of the way the world is independent of the mind would be desirable if we could get it, but we probably cannot get it. However, Williams thinks that not only is the ACR desirable, but it must be possible to achieve it because we've already made considerable progress in doing so. Williams argues that the convergence of opinion in some domains, notably, the natural sciences, is good reason to think that the object of those opinions is something mind-independent. If many different people with different points of view agree in an opinion, their opinion is probably about something independent of their various points of view (pp. 242–45). The convergence of opinion does not *prove* that the opinion is part of the ACR, but it is good reason to think that it is. So Williams thinks that the ACR must be a possible thing to construct because we are already constructing it. We can keep the ACR and still avoid radical skepticism.

Of course, many people are not so sanguine about the prospects for succeeding at constructing a conception of reality independent of the mind. If they feel the skeptical lure inherent in the ACR, they may conclude that the conception itself must be rejected. In the rest of this chapter we will investigate some interesting ways to reject the ACR. In considering whether we should reject the idea that the object of knowledge is something independent of the mind, try not to confuse the position that we *cannot* successfully construct the ACR from the quite different position that we *wouldn't care* about the ACR. It is possible for a person to have both positions, but they are distinct.

II. O. K. BOUWSMA AND THE EVIL GENIUS

Let us begin with a simple and very enjoyable paper by O. K. Bouwsma called "Descartes' Evil Genius" (1965). I interpret Bouwsma's position against skepticism as partly metaphysical and partly semantic. In this section I will summarize Bouwsma's argument, since it is a good take-off for a number of important positions against skepticism, but you will want to read the paper yourself since it is so much fun.

Bouwsma argues in the form of a narrative about a human being, Tom, and the Evil Genius. At the beginning of the story Tom lives in a world like you and I inhabit—a physical world that includes tables, flowers, and his beloved Millie. The nefarious Evil Genius (EG) first undertakes a rather feeble bit of mischief. He changes all physical objects in Tom's environment into paper. Tom's paper body lives in a paper house and Millie talks from a paper mouth, and there are paper flowers on a paper table. However, Tom is not fooled for long. He sees through the illusion created by the EG and realizes that everything is made of paper. Bouwsma's point in this first scenario is to establish what it would take for something to be an illusion. "An illusion is something that looks like or sounds like, so much like, something else that you either mistake it for something else, or you can easily understand how someone might come to do this" (p. 89). Bouwsma claims that paper flowers are an illusion for Tom only if Tom can tell the difference between flowers and paper. Nothing is an illusion unless it is detectable. Tom *can* tell the difference between flowers and paper, so the paper world is an illusion, but it is an illusion that Tom discovers.

Bouwsma then moves on to the second scenario in which the EG gets bolder and destroys even the paper world. On the second day of the EG's meddling, nothing is left but Tom's mind and the EG himself. The EG does such a good job of it that Tom does not notice any difference, and the EG is sorely vexed. "To deceive but to be unsuspected is too little glory" (pp. 92–93). So the EG plants the seeds of doubt in Tom's mind. When Tom stops to admire the flowers in the vase, the EG whispers into his mind's ear, "Flowers? Flowers? Are you sure?" And getting too little doubt by way of response, the EG reveals his great deception. But Tom is unmoved.

"My flowers illusions?" exclaimed Tom, and he took up the bowl and placed it before a mirror. "See," said he, "here are the flowers and here, in the mirror, is an illusion. There's a difference surely. And you with my eyes, my nose, and my fingers can tell what that difference is.... I can tell flowers from illusions, and my flowers, as you now plainly see, are not illusions." (p. 94)

In frustration the EG insists that the flowers in front of the mirror are illusory.

> "Tom," he said, "notice. The flowers in the mirror look like flowers, but they only look like flowers. We agree about that. The flowers before the mirror also look like flowers. But they, you say, are flowers because they also smell like flowers and they feel like flowers.... Imagine a mirror such that it reflected not only the looks of flowers, but also their fragrance and petal surfaces, and then you smelled and touched, and the flowers before the mirror would be just like the flowers in the mirror. Then you could see immediately that the flowers before the mirror are illusions, just as those in the mirror are illusions. As it is now, it is clear that the flowers in the mirror are thin illusions, and the flowers before the mirror are thick. Thick illusions are the best for deception." (p. 95)

Tom is still unfazed: "I see that what you mean by thin illusions is what I mean by illusions, and what you mean by thick illusions is what I mean by flowers. So when you say that my flowers are your thick illusions this doesn't bother me" (p. 95).

The EG now explains all. He has a sense, *cerpicio*, which is denied to Tom, and which permits him to distinguish real from illusory flowers. He cannot *cerpicio* the flowers before the mirror, so the flowers before the mirror are not real flowers. Tom replies that it does not matter whether his flowers can be *cerpicioed* or not, since what he means by "flowers" is not defined by reference to a sense he does not have. "If your intention was to deceive, you must learn the language of those you are to deceive," says Tom (p. 96).

Bouwsma concludes that the Evil Genius fails to deceive Tom. Tom's world is not illusory. His belief that he is looking at flowers is true and he is not deceived. That is because our words are used to refer to items of our experience. As long as the experience remains the same, the reference does also. If the reference remains the same, so does the truth of the belief. When Tom says "These are beautiful flowers" after the EG has destroyed the physical world, he is saying the same thing he said the day before, and what he says remains true. The EG hypothesis thus fails to lead to skepticism.

I interpret Bouwsma's position here as partly semantic because it is a view about the reference of words, but it is also metaphysical because I think Bouwsma wants to say that Tom lives in the same world after the EG destroys the material world as he did before. The

EG *cannot* destroy Tom's world. Even though the EG can destroy matter, the EG cannot fool Tom into massive and undetectable errors. An undetectable error is not an error; there is no illusion.

Has Bouwsma succeeded in undermining the point of the Evil Genius scenario? Let's suppose that we take Bouwsma's second story at face value, that is, the EG really does what he says he does. What follows?

First, I think we should admit that something is different in the world around Tom than the day before the EG did his dirty work. When Tom has the experience he would describe as standing before a table holding a vase of flowers, it is not the case that what is standing before him then is the same thing as what was standing before him the day before. It can't be because the EG destroyed what was there the day before. That means that if Tom should say:

T1: What I see here before me now is identical to what I saw before me yesterday,

he would be speaking falsely. Whether or not we want to call this an illusion depends upon what we mean by an illusion. I would call it an illusion and Bouwsma would not, but I don't think the meaning of "illusion" is essential to Descartes's point. As long as Tom is speaking falsely, he is clearly making a mistake. The EG has fooled Tom into thinking that T1 is true when it is in fact false.

Now you might think that nobody ever senses anything outside their minds. Maybe even when there *was* a physical world, Tom never saw it or felt it or smelled it. There always was a barrier between Tom's mind and the outside world. What Tom sensed was in his mind even when there was also a world outside his mind. If so, T1 is true and Bouwsma is right. The EG has not deceived Tom by destroying the physical world.

But in that case the EG would know there is a barrier and would have no reason to even try to deceive Tom. If he tries, he not only fails, he is stupid. On the assumption that Tom never experiences anything but his own mind, Bouwsma's story permits the truth of T1, but only because the EG does not understand the relation between Tom's mind and the world. What kind of evil "genius" is that? On the other hand, if the EG is right about the relation between Tom's mind and the world, Tom is in error if he asserts T1.

Now let us suppose that Tom makes a further statement:

T2: These are the same flowers I saw yesterday.

61

If Tom's belief T1 is false, I think we should conclude that T2 is false also. But the truth or falsehood of T2 depends upon what "flowers" refers to. How are we to decide that?

Since none of us can imagine what *cerpicio* is like (nor can Bouwsma since he just made up the word), let's consider a thought experiment using a sense with which we are all familiar. Suppose we lacked the sense of smell but everything in our world was the same as it is now. Would "flowers" refer to what looks and feels like flowers, but not what smells like flowers? If we gained the sense of smell would we say, "Oh, flowers smell nice"? I think so, but would that change the meaning of "flowers"? Would "flowers" now refer to something different than it did before? Would we now be speaking a different language, one in which things are defined, in part, by reference to the way they smell? I think not.

But let's make the story closer to Bouwsma's. Imagine that due to an ecological disaster that occurred two hundred years ago, no one in the world today has or ever has had the sense of smell except one woman who was spared by an enormous stroke of luck. Imagine that everything else about this world is the same as ours. In particular, it contains flowers and people use the word "flowers" the same way we do except that they cannot smell the flowers. Now suppose the EG enters the scene and destroys all flowers, putting in their place an excellent imitation of flowers. In fact, these "flowers" are such an excellent imitation of the real thing that they can only be detected as fakes by the sense of smell. The woman with the sense of smell says to everyone, "These aren't flowers. They smell like gasoline." It is doubtful that other people would be convinced by her puzzling talk about the way things smell, but if suddenly everybody else gained the sense of smell, would they say, "Ah, now we see that you were right; these aren't flowers"? It is hard to answer this question because we may not think that the sense of smell detects essential properties of an object, and if it does, those properties would be detectable by other senses as well, so the thought experiment is not applicable to the world with the laws of nature our world has.

But here is a thought experiment using something that actually happened. Beginning in the seventies an important theory of reference emerged in the work of Saul Kripke (1980), Hilary Putnam (1975), and others. One of the focuses of their theory was natural kind terms like "water." The term "water" was used long before anything was known about molecular theory and, in particular, before it was known that water is H_2O. However, now we simply do not count anything as water unless it is H_2O even if it would have been mistaken for water in the past. So even though "water" was introduced into English by way of certain observed qualities of taste and appearance, if we came across anything that had exactly the right qualities of taste and appearance but wasn't H_2O, we would say it is "illusory water." That means that the stuff that appeared exactly the same as water on the macroscopic level was not water even before it was possible to detect that it was not H_2O. The invention of the microscope did not actually give us a new sense, but it did extend a sense we already had. Kripke argued that after the seventeenth century we had a new and superior way of determining whether something is water, but that in no way changed the meaning of the word "water." "Water" always referred to "that stuff," where the nature of that stuff was open for investigation. We think that molecular structure is part of the deep nature of that stuff, and so the discovery that water is H_2O was a discovery about the nature of something we were talking about all along.

Now let's consider Bouwsma's imaginary sense of *cerpicio*. If there was such a thing as *cerpicio* and some things we call "flowers" did not pass the *cerpicio* test, would we think that they are not really flowers, just as we say now that anything that is not H_2O is not really water? I think we would say that only if we also think that what passes the *cerpicio* test is connected to the deep nature of flowers. But on what grounds would we think that? We think the molecular structure of water is part of its deep nature because the development of molecular theory permitted us to form a conception of the physical world according to which molecular structure underlies ordinary sensory properties and explains them. So the use of the microscope permitted us to add a refinement to the ordinary conception of water. *Cerpicio* is different. Not only do we lack such a sense, but it may be necessary that we lack it because *cerpicio* may be incompatible with human nature, so it is not even possible for us to adapt the results of the use of *cerpicio* to our ordinary conception of water. If *cerpicio* reveals the deep nature of flowers, it cannot be because our own future science would lead us to that conclusion.

But what difference does it make whether we can acquire the sense of *cerpicio*? As long as the flowers before and after the EG's intervention *cerpicio* differently, surely there is *some* important difference between them, even if Tom cannot detect it. But Bouwsma could amend his story to strengthen his case. Suppose the EG destroyed flowers before language was invented. Imagine that "flowers" entered the language when there were only flower images, so

Tom was always living in a world of images, not physical objects. My objection that T1 and T2 are false would not apply to the amended story, and Bouwsma's answer to the EG would be stronger.

But notice that in the amended story, the EG would know that future humans like Tom will be living forever in a world of images, so there is no difference between the amended scenario and a world in which no physical objects ever existed, a world that always was a world of images. In both cases Tom might be deceived in what he believes about the world, but the EG does not get credit for Tom's mistake. Of course, that does not mean the skeptic loses the argument. It just means that skepticism is not really a worry about what the EG does. It is a worry about what the world of our experience is really like. Perhaps we are living in a world of images, and perhaps we always have been. If we accept the Absolute Conception of Reality and there is nothing that is "there anyway," we would be living under an illusion.

The ACR makes skepticism threatening because of the gap between the mind and the world we seek to know. Descartes thought the gap can be bridged by attention to features of the mind itself, but most subsequent philosophers thought he was unsuccessful. George Berkeley closed the gap from the other end: He argued that the world we know is in our minds, the position of metaphysical **Idealism**. Idealists deny (2) of the ACR, and one of the most compelling reasons to accept Idealism is its escape from the skeptical threat of the ACR.

Bouwsma could be interpreted as a Berkeleyan Idealist. Bouwsma does not deny the existence of a physical world, but he argues for a view of reference according to which our words refer to the immediate objects of experience whether or not there is a world outside our minds. That is the point of arguing that Tom refers to the same thing both before and after the physical world is destroyed by the EG. Bouwsma's position does not necessarily commit him to Idealism, then, because it is compatible with the existence of an external physical world, but if there is such a world, we do not refer to it in our language. Its existence would be superfluous. In my opinion that is a high price to pay to avoid skepticism. However, Idealism has a distinguished history in philosophy and its avoidance of skepticism is one of its attractions.

In the next section we will look at another way to use semantics to argue against the skeptic.

III. PUTNAM AND THE BRAIN-IN-A-VAT

Let us return to Putnam and Kripke's theory of natural kind terms. In Putnam's famous paper "The Meaning of 'Meaning,'" he argued that two common assumptions about meaning and reference cannot both be true: (i) The reference of a term is determined by its meaning, and (ii) meanings are in the head.[3] A simplified version of the view to which he is objecting goes like this: The meaning of a kind term like "elm tree" is a description, in this case, a description of an elm tree, and when a person grasps the meaning of "elm tree" the person has that description in her head. When she says "elm" she refers to whatever it is in the world that satisfies that description.

Putnam's well-known thought experiments are intended to show that this cannot be the way it works. In one example, Putnam reveals that he cannot tell the difference between an elm tree and a beech tree. In other words, the description he associates in his head with "elm tree" is exactly the same as the one he associates with "beech tree." Yet surely he can successfully refer to elm trees and to beech trees, and he can successfully form beliefs about them. For instance, he might believe that the elm trees in his neighborhood are dying because he read about it in the local newspaper, and he does not believe that the beech trees are dying. If he successfully refers to elm trees by using the word "elm" without the appropriate descriptive meaning in his head, then it cannot be what is in his head that determines that to which he refers. Either meaning does not determine reference, or as Putnam says, "meanings ain't in the head." One moral of this thought experiment is that Putnam succeeds at referring to elm trees because he relies on other people who *can* distinguish elm trees from other kinds of tree, so reference has a social dimension. Putnam refers to elm trees because he is linked up to elm trees through a causal process that goes through other people.

According to Putnam, it is important that there are actually elm trees, not something else, at the other end of the causal connection when Putnam says "elm tree." His "Twin Earth" thought experiment is meant to convince you of that. Suppose there is a planet just like Earth except that the chemical constitution of the stuff that looks like water is not H_2O, which does not even exist on Twin Earth, but is something else, which we can call XYZ. On Twin Earth, "water"

---

[3] Putnam (1975). See also Putnam (1981), especially the first chapter, "Brain-in-a-Vat."

would refer to XYZ, not to H_2O, even though the idea in the minds of the Twin Earthians would be exactly the same as the idea in the minds of the people on Earth. That is, the Twin Earthians would have exactly the same idea we have of an odorless, colorless liquid that is drinkable and fills the lakes and streams, so their mental states when they think "water" are the same as ours even though they refer to something different in their external environment. If this is right, the idea in the head does not determine the reference in the world.

Putnam's paper and others published at about the same time began a movement called **externalism in the philosophy of mind** (not be confused with externalism in epistemology, discussed in Chapter Two).[4] It is externalist because the content of concepts is given by something external to the mind, and the way language refers to items in the world is not determined by what is in the mind. Thoughts in the head do not intrinsically refer to anything. They refer because the referrer has an ability to refer acquired through a causal process linking her through her linguistic community to the thing to which she is referring. You cannot have water thoughts without water out there to which you are causally connected. The Twin Earthians refer to XYZ and the Earthians refer to H_2O when they say or think "water."

Putnam uses his externalist semantical theory to argue against Cartesian skepticism:

Putnam's Argument against Skepticism

(1) Suppose I am a brain in a vat that is being stimulated by a mischievous scientist into thinking I have seen trees, although I have never seen a tree. I have no contact with a physical world.

(2) Then my word "tree" refers not to what non-vat people call "trees," but to whatever the scientist uses to produce the stimulus that causes me to think, "There's a tree." "Tree" refers to tree images or electrical impulses in my brain, or something of the sort. In any case, it does not refer to physical trees because I have no causal connection to physical trees. Just as the inhabitants of Twin Earth

---

[4] These influential papers include Putnam (1975), Kripke (1980), and Burge (1979). Since then there have been many more papers on externalism such as Dretzke (1995), Tye (1995), and Brueckner (1992).

refer to XYZ, not water, when they think "water," vat inhabitants refer to something other than trees when they think "tree." When I think "There is a tree" I am usually thinking something true.

(3) So I cannot use the word "tree" to form the thought that the scientist would express by saying I have never seen a tree. Similarly, I cannot use the word "material object" to form the thought that I've never seen a material object, nor can I use the word "vat" to form the thought that maybe I'm a brain in a vat. The scientist and I are using different languages. I use vat English. The scientist uses English.

(4) So if I were a brain in a vat, my word "vat" would not refer to vats (what the scientist calls a "vat"), but to vat images or the electrical stimuli that give me the images. If I think, "Maybe I'm a brain in a vat," my thought would be false.

(5) Therefore, the skeptical position is impossible since if it were true, it would be false. The conditions of reference permit us to think maybe there are no trees or that we are brains in a vat only if it is not true. (Putnam, 1981)

Let us look at (2) for a moment. You might object that even assuming Putnam's externalist theory is correct, since the vat designer is in the causal chain leading to my image of a tree, and since the vat designer has seen real trees, real trees are in the causal chain leading to my (the vat inhabitant's) word "tree." The same point applies to the rest of my referring expressions, including "brain" and "vat." But Putnam could reply that in the vat, physical objects are not in the causal chain in the right way. Think of it this way. If God created the world and had certain ideas in his mind that he used as patterns for what he created, we would *not* say that our words refer to those forms in God's mind. Analogously, if the nefarious scientist put you in a vat and created images of trees and brains and vats and other physical objects in your brain, we should not say that your words "tree," and "brain," and "vat" refer to what the scientist uses as the pattern for the images he produces in you. Of course, this response does not tell us what it takes to be causally connected in the right way, but it suggests that Putnam's account of reference in the vat has a lot of intuitive force, provided that you accept his externalist semantical theory.

Notice, however, that Putnam's account does not seem to give an antiskeptical result if I was only recently envatted. That is because the reference of my words "vat," "brain," and so on would refer to physical brains and vats if I learned and used my language during the time I was living in a physical world. I claimed above that Bouwsma's argument makes more sense if the EG destroyed the physical world before I learned language, and for the same reason it is more plausible if the physical world never existed. It seems to me that Putnam's argument also is stronger if I was not put into a vat recently. In fact, I don't think the argument is at all plausible against that possibility. How does Putnam's argument compare with Bouwsma's argument in other respects? Both of them rely upon a view of reference, although Bouwsma's semantical position is not developed. Bouwsma maintains (without argument in that paper, as far as I can tell) that the referent of a term is essentially tied to items in the mind, so either no physical world exists, or the physical world is superfluous in that it is beyond our experience and is not the world we talk about. Bouwsma would reject the Absolute Conception of Reality as described by Williams and attributed to Descartes. Bouwsma's answer to Descartes, then, is to reject the idea that the object of knowledge is mind-independent. I don't think Bouwsma's position is that we *cannot* form the conception of a mind-independent reality, reality as experienced by the Evil Genius. After all, Bouwsma wrote the story himself and must have thought of himself as conceiving of the Evil Genius's predicament. But Bouwsma's point is that *that* is not a conception of the object of human knowledge.

Bouwsma does not deny that meanings are in the head, nor does he deny that the meaning of a term like "flowers" determines the reference. But the referent of "flowers" is in the head too. In contrast, Putnam argues that if the referent of a term is determined by the meaning, then neither the referent nor the meaning is in the head. The object of knowledge is mind-independent, but then so is the content of one's concepts. This is a very interesting way to reject the ACR. The object of knowledge is not independent of the state of knowing, but that is not because the object of knowledge is in the head, but because both the object of knowing and the contents of one's thoughts are external to the mind.

The Absolute Conception of Reality threatens skepticism because it separates mind and world, so it raises the issue of the relation between our thoughts and experiences, on the one hand,

and the world we seek to know on the other. Idealists bridge the gap between mind and world by moving the world into the mind. The object of knowledge is a world of experience, where experience is understood as something that goes on in the mind. Putnam bridges the gap between mind and world by moving many of the contents of the mind into the world. What we are thinking and experiencing is not something that goes on in the mind, but is something that, at least in part, goes on in the world. Both approaches seek to block skepticism by questioning the conception of mind and reality pre-supposed in the skeptical scenarios.

Does Putnam's semantic externalism avoid skepticism? Thomas Nagel (1986, p. 72) argues that even if Putnam's argument is sound and terms like "vat" and "brain" when used in the vat fail to refer to vats and brains, Putnam has not succeeded in avoiding skepticism since all the skeptic needs to do is to express his skepticism in different terms. He can say, "Perhaps I can't even *think* the truth about what I am because I lack the necessary concepts and my circumstances make it impossible to acquire them." Nagel remarks that if that is not skepticism, he doesn't know what is (p. 72).

I think that Nagel's objection reveals an important way in which skeptical doubts are immune to the moves of Putnam, Bouwsma, and the Idealists. Skepticism is not really about brains in vats any more than Descartes's skepticism is about the Evil Genius. The problem is that our experience is compatible with our being very different sorts of beings than we imagine. We could be Buddhist selves, or part of the World Soul, or any of indefinitely many other things. And like-wise, what we call the world could be very different from anything we can imagine. The real lesson of skepticism is not that we might be a *particular* sort of nonhuman being, or a human being who is manipulated in some particular way, but that we might be very far from understanding what kind of beings we are and what the world is really like. This possibility is something we should take seriously because there *are* skeptics in this sense, whereas nobody believes she is a brain-in-a-vat (BIV). Notice, however, that this is not really fair as a rejoinder to Putnam, since Putnam took himself to be replying to the Cartesian skeptic who assumes that we *can* form thoughts about what we are—a BIV or something of the sort.

It seems to me, however, that there is another problem with using externalism about concepts to answer the skeptic. Putnam removes the veil between thoughts and reality implicit in the Abso-lute Conception of Reality, but he veils the mind's access to its own thoughts, arguably an even worse kind of skepticism.[5] When I think the thought I express by saying, "The elm trees in my neighborhood are dying," the content of my thought is determined by the trees outside my mind. Both the object of reference of my word "elm" and the thought I have about elm trees is independent of my mind. There is a sense in which I don't know what I am thinking when I think that the elm trees are dying. Similarly, if I were a BIV and think "Maybe I am a BIV," Putnam argues that the thought I have is not the same as the thought that you and I have when we entertain that possibility right now. But the fact that my thought in the vat is a thought about vat images or electrical stimuli in my brain rather than a thought about brains and vats is not accessible to my consciousness. And so, I don't know what thought I'm thinking when I think "Maybe I am a BIV." Am I thinking a thought about brains and vats or am I thinking a thought about brain images and vat images or something else entirely? I escape skepticism about truth at the price of getting skepticism about my own thoughts.

What should a conscientious believer think about skepticism? I argued in Chapter One that we commit ourselves to believing conscientiously about the things we care about, so if it is important to us that we are more or less the way we think we are and the world is more or less the way we think it is, we commit ourselves to having conscientious beliefs about the way we are and the way the world is. I also argued that the more we care, the more conscientious we must be and the greater the demand on us that we be conscientious. Some responses to skepticism are responses to skepticism about knowledge. That is, given reliabilism or contextualism or the denial of the closure principle, we do not need to *know* we are not brains in vats in order to know most of the things we think we know about ourselves and the world.

But as we've seen, skepticism threatens more than knowledge; it threatens conscientious belief. The standards for conscientious belief differ from the standards for knowledge. It is not necessarily more difficult to have a conscientious belief than to have knowledge. In fact, in at least one way, it is easier to have the former than the latter: Knowledge requires true belief and conscientiousness does not. But a

---

[5] Paul Boghossian (1997) and Michael McKinsey (1991) argue for the incompatibility of externalism of mental content and first-person privileged authority with respect to one's current mental states. Tyler Burge (1988), Brian McLaughlin and Michael Tye (1998), John Heil (1988), and others have argued that the two are compatible.

belief might satisfy some criteria for knowledge but not conscientious belief. At the end of Chapter Two I argued that even if contextualism, reliabilism, or the denial of epistemic closure answers the skeptical threat to knowledge, these positions are much less plausible as answers to the skeptical threat to conscientious belief. In the final section of this chapter we will return to the epistemically conscientious person and will look at the relationship between conscientious belief and self-trust.

IV. SKEPTICISM, SELF-TRUST, AND CONSCIENTIOUS BELIEF

Human beings have many faculties and capacities by means of which we attempt to connect to the world. In addition to perceptual and epistemic faculties, we have emotions, and we make choices and act for ends. The conscientious person aims to exercise each of these faculties or capacities in a way that makes an accurate or appropriate connection to the world. So we not only aim to have accurate perceptions and true beliefs, but we also aim to have appropriate emotions—to admire the admirable, fear the fearsome, pity the pitiful, and so on, and we also aim to choose what is good and to act in a way that succeeds in reaching ends appropriate for the circumstances. To be conscientious in the broadest sense is try to make all of our connections to the world as appropriate as we can make them. To be epistemically conscientious is to try to make our epistemic connections as appropriate as we can make them, which means we try to make our beliefs true and we try to have true beliefs.

As we saw in Chapter One, these two aims are not the same. Both aims are included in epistemic conscientiousness because there are two ways we can fail to connect to reality through our belief-forming capacities: (1) We can connect to the wrong thing by having a false belief, or (2) we can fail to connect by not having a belief. In Chapter One I argued that we commit ourselves to having conscientious beliefs in the domains we care about as well as in the domain of morality, a domain about which caring is not optional. In such domains we commit ourselves to trying to ensure that the beliefs we have in those domains are true rather than false, and we commit ourselves to trying to acquire true beliefs in those domains.

The skeptic argues that we ought to doubt a vast number of our beliefs, including beliefs in domains we care about. Doubt that p is a state of mind that undermines the motive to believe p. Skepticism thus attacks conscientious belief by undermining the motive of a conscientious believer to believe. The skeptical arguments we have considered purport to show us that we ought to either give up or to weaken the degree to which we believe many of our beliefs. That is the conscientious thing to do if the skeptical arguments succeed in showing us that these beliefs may be false. But in moving from belief to doubt we are either moving from believing what is true to doubt, or we are moving from believing what is false to doubt. If it is the former, we lose the right connection to reality. If it is the latter, we move from one way of failing to connect to reality to another. Believing what is false is one way to fail to connect to reality; doubting is another. When we look at doubt from this point of view, doubt may not be the conscientious epistemic stance.

But doubt can be an epistemic improvement over false belief. That is because doubt is often a stage in between believing what is false and believing what is true; moving from false belief to true belief often goes through doubt. But what if a person gets stuck at the stage of doubt? That might still be an improvement because at least she will not act on false beliefs. Recall Clifford's story of the ship owner who sent his ship full of emigrants to sea, believing without evidence that his ship was seaworthy. The belief was false and the ship went down, but if the ship owner had doubted his belief, presumably he would have been less inclined to send the ship to its doom. A conscientious person has conscientious beliefs about the potential consequences of her acts and does not act on beliefs that are not conscientiously held when the consequences may be serious. So a person who doubts may be more conscientious than one who does not.

But doubt can also undermine conscientiousness. Since acts depend upon beliefs, we cannot act conscientiously without believing conscientiously, and we cannot believe conscientiously if we do not believe. If the skeptic is right, we cannot trust our epistemic faculties, but we cannot trust our other faculties either. If we cannot trust that our beliefs are true, how can we trust that what we fear or love or pity is worthy of fear or love or pity, and how can we trust that our choices are correct on any measure of correctness—correctness by the standards of God or the standards of our community, or even by our own standards? If I cannot trust that my beliefs about an external world are true, I cannot trust that my beliefs about what is a worthy object of choice are true. And if I can't trust that my beliefs about what is a worthy object of choice are true, why should I choose what I choose?

The parallel point applies to beliefs about what is a fitting object of emotions. If I cannot trust that my beliefs about what is admirable are true, why should I admire those whom I admire? So if we have grounds for skepticism about beliefs, we also have grounds for skepticism about emotions and choices. Emotions and choices, like beliefs, are ways of being connected to an external world, and doubts about the existence or nature of that world infect the appropriateness or correctness of our emotions and choices. Since skepticism undermines conscientious belief by undermining belief, skepticism also undermines conscientious action, emotion, and choice by undermining the grounds for action, emotion, and choice.

Skepticism undermines human agency by undermining the exercise of normal human faculties of believing and choosing. I assume that a conscientious person does not permit her agency to be undermined, yet we may not see how to answer the skeptic, whose argument, if taken in full seriousness, leads to the undermining of agency. We cannot live a normal life, much less a flourishing life, without a substantial amount of trust in the general reliability of our faculties. That means we must reject skepticism, whether or not we accept any given response to skepticism as adequate. But we must go farther than that. Even if we think we have an adequate response to radical skepticism, that is not enough to give us epistemic support for a normal life since there is a big gap between the rejection of skepticism and the establishment of the positive thesis that our ordinary faculties generally connect us to reality in an accurate or appropriate way. So even if we think we are justified in believing that we are not living in a virtual reality machine, that is a far cry from giving us confidence in the wide range of beliefs needed to live a good life.

We will never be able to get evidence that our human faculties in general give us appropriate connections to reality. It would be impossible to get such evidence. I think that means that the need for self-trust arises at a fundamental level in the life of a rational agent. Self-trust is not sufficient for conscientiousness, however, because the use of a conscientious person's faculties shows her the advantage of conscientious believing and choosing. She observes that conscientious persons more often get it right than those who are not conscientious, where the identification of conscientious and unconscientious persons and the observation of what they do and whether they get it right is done by the conscientious exercise of her own faculties. From the perspective of one conscientiously using her faculties, conscientious persons are more reliable than unconscientious persons. In contrast, unconscientious persons are less reliable even from their own perspective. In Chapter Four we will turn to the virtues of the conscientious person and the implications of self-trust.

My response to skepticism is that we have the same grounds for rejecting it as we have for taking it seriously in the first place. Skepticism arises from the belief that there is a gap between the mind and the world. We have no argument for that belief, but it is natural. It is equally natural to believe the gap can be bridged. That belief, I've argued, is reasonable, and because we have that belief, we need self-trust. Self-trust is reasonable in the sense that it is unreasonable to permit reason to thwart our nature. The person who takes skepticism seriously enough to let it affect her confidence in a wide range of her beliefs, emotions, and acts is a person who permits reason to thwart her nature. It is not reasonable to do that even if the use of reason does not show us a convincing response to the infinite regress argument or Cartesian skepticism.

This reply to skepticism does not apply to those skeptics whose type of skepticism permits them to lead a normal, flourishing life. Above I observed that skepticism is not really about brains in vats; it is about the possibility that what we are and what the world is like might be radically different from what we take it to be. So a Buddhist who believes the ordinary conception of a separable self is an illusion and that most of what we naturally believe is illusory has as radically skeptical a view of himself and the world as the skeptic who believes the BIV hypothesis. But unlike the BIV skeptic, the Buddhist is not *only* a skeptic about ordinary beliefs. He has many beliefs about the true nature of the world and himself, and a life based on the tenets of Buddhism can be flourishing, sometimes more flourishing than a life based on commonsense beliefs about the self and the world.

My claim that self-trust is reasonable also may not apply to the Pyrrhonian skeptic who finds the lack of the need to make judgments liberating. I do not know if there are any Pyrrhonian skeptics, but there might be. Is a Pyrrhonian skeptic an agent? Does she act on reasons? Does she make choices and plan for the future? I have no idea how one can live a normal, flourishing life without making any judgments, but if it is possible to do so, then my position does not count against such a person's skepticism.

There is another response that the skeptic can make to my argument. She might agree that epistemic self-trust is a psychological necessity for the epistemically conscientious agent, while denying that self-trust is epistemically conscientious, given one or more skeptical argument. But the epistemically conscientious person just *is* a person whose beliefs are motivated by epistemic considerations, including those advanced by the skeptic. To the extent that the epistemically conscientious agent accepts that a belief *p* is epistemically unconscientious, her motive to believe *p* is undermined. She cannot continue to believe *p* while simultaneously accepting the success of the skeptical argument against the epistemic conscientiousness of believing *p*. She can recognize the psychological necessity of epistemic self-trust in others, but to the extent that accepts the skeptic's argument, that psychological necessity does not apply to herself. She must either become a Pyrrhonian skeptic, if she can, or she must reject the success of the skeptical argument against the epistemic conscientiousness of her beliefs.

I would like to end this chapter with an observation about a peculiarity of my use of the idea of being epistemically conscientious. I have been treating conscientiousness in beliefs as comparable to conscientiousness in acts. I assume that we are capable of being conscientious in believing, which means that we must be able to exercise enough control over the acquisition and revision of our beliefs that we can respond to warnings against bullshit, against believing the way Clifford's ship owner believed, against taking skepticism seriously enough to undermine the trust we need to live a normal life, and so on. That means I am assuming a controversial view called **doxastic voluntarism**, the position that our beliefs are under our control. It is pretty clear that some of our beliefs are not under our control, and others are only under our control indirectly. I think the model I am using does no harm as long as we realize that I am exaggerating the control we have over our beliefs because what a being with total control over her beliefs would do tells us something important about what a being with less control should do. The perfectly conscientious person with perfect control over her beliefs is a kind of ideal—not in the sense that we would want to be such a person, but in the sense that helps us see more clearly what beings like us should do, if we can. It is possible to be epistemically conscientious, and an epistemically conscientious person has a better life epistemically. It seems to me that an epistemically better life is likely to be a better life, period. We will discuss that in the last chapter.

Among the many desires we have by nature is a desire for knowledge, as well as desires for happiness, love, and freedom from domination and the objects of our fears. Skepticism is the permanent lack of confidence in the satisfiability of our natural desire for knowledge, truth, or other epistemic goods. We have no guarantee that our natural epistemic desires can be satisfied, and neither do we have any guarantee that our other natural desires can be satisfied. The question "What do we desire and can we get it?" is really no different in epistemology than it is in ethics. The second conjunct can be answered skeptically, but it is best answered by attending to human nature.

FURTHER READING

Although the kind of skepticism discussed in this chapter is implicit in a variety of epistemological writings, epistemology texts generally do not deal with it directly because it overlaps the field of metaphysics. The best start would be to read some of the primary sources, including Bernard Arthur Owen Williams's *Descartes: The Project of Pure Enquiry* (Atlantic Highlands, NJ: Humanities Press, 1978) and O. K. Bouwsma's essay "Descartes' Evil Genius" in his *Philosophical Essays* (Lincoln: University of Nebraska Press, 1965). The issues in this chapter can be found throughout the writings of the modern era from Descartes to Kant, and in the many forms of post-Kantian Idealism. Roger Ariew and Eric Watkins (eds.), *Modern Philosophy: An Anthology of Primary Sources* (Indianapolis, IN: Hackett Publishing Co., 1998) contains an array of classic essays from early modern philosophers. Semantic approaches to skepticism can be found in Keith DeRose and Ted Warfield (eds.), *Skepticism: A Contemporary Reader* (Oxford: Oxford University Press, 1999), which includes Hilary Putnam's classic paper "Brains-in-a-Vat." For an influential paper on the new theory of reference, advanced students may want to read Saul Kripke's *Naming and Necessity* (Cambridge, MA: Harvard University Press, 1980).

4

Trust and the Intellectual Virtues

I. EPISTEMIC SELF-TRUST AND THE VIRTUES THAT REGULATE IT

A. Conscientious Self-Trust

The American pragmatist philosopher John Dewey relates an amusing anecdote in one of his works in educational theory: "The story is told of a man in slight repute for intelligence, who, desiring to be chosen selectman in his New England town, addressed a knot of neighbors in this wise: 'I hear that you don't believe I know enough to hold office. I wish you to understand that I am thinking about something or other most of the time.'"[1] We are all thinking about something or other most of the time, just as we are all doing something or other most of the time. Unfortunately, that does not mean that we are always thinking well any more than it means we are always acting well. Most of the time we do not do a very impressive job at either one.

Nonetheless, we can try. In this chapter we will look more carefully at what the conscientious thinker does. At the end of the last chapter we concluded our discussion of skepticism with an argument for epistemic self-trust. In this chapter we will begin with self-trust

---

[1] Dewey (1933), p. 4.

and will explore its implications for trust in others. We will look at some of the virtues that enhance or restrain self-trust or trust in the members of our epistemic communities, and then we will examine a puzzling conflict between trust in self and trust in others: How should we respond when there is irresolvable disagreement in belief between ourselves and people we epistemically admire?

In Chapter Three we examined a serious form of skepticism that arises from the belief that there is a gap between our minds and the world we seek to grasp. It is quite possible that this belief is natural in the sense that it is almost universal, or at any rate, very common, and that might be a sufficient reason to take it seriously; but even so, I think that there is also a natural belief that the gap can be bridged. The skeptic accepts the first belief but not the second. My position is that it is just as reasonable to accept the second as the first. We do not have evidence for either one, but, then, we would have to be very confused to expect such evidence. How could we ever find out that our minds and the world are separated? How could we ever find out that our faculties taken as a whole reliably put us in contact with that world?

On the other hand, we do have circular evidence—evidence using our faculties—that our faculties are typically reliable, and we also have evidence that they are sometimes mistaken. We know that because we check the use of our faculties by using other faculties or by using the same faculty on another occasion. If I'm not sure I see a spider on the carpet, I take a closer look. If I'm not sure I left my keys on the kitchen counter, I go and look or ask someone else to do so. If I'm not sure that the local election is next week, I ask other people. So we check a perception by another perception or testimony; we check our memory by perception, other memories, and testimony; we check testimony by perception and memory, and so on. None of our faculties can be demonstrated to be reliable from outside the use of those faculties, but we can check particular uses of our faculties by using some of our other faculties or the same faculty again.[2]

That means we need self-trust in those faculties that we think lead us to the truth. What I mean by self-trust is the state of having

---

[2] Richard Foley (2001) makes this point about our faculties and beliefs taken as a whole. William Alston (1991) makes a similar point about basic faculties and the practices in which they are embedded. Alston's point is stronger because he argues that there is more than one basic epistemic practice the reliability of which cannot be determined in a noncircular way. Perceptual practice is one such practice. Memory is another. I think Alston's point is correct, but most of what I say in this book uses only the weaker point that we have no noncircular way to determine the reliability of our faculties as a whole.

the same confidence we would have if, *per impossibile*, we had non-circular support for the belief that our faculties are reliable as a whole. Even though we lack such support, we act as if we had it, and we have the same attitude toward our faculties that we would have if we had proof of their reliability. We live our lives with the belief that truth is within our grasp, and we assume that we know what the faculties are that get us to the truth, at least some of them. They include our perceptual faculties, memory, and cognitive faculties.

Somewhat more controversially, I think, they include emotions. Emotion dispositions can be reliable or unreliable, and particular emotions may fit or not fit their objects.[3] But we cannot tell whether our emotion dispositions are reliable without using those same dispositions in conjunction with our other faculties. We cannot tell whether our disposition to pity is reliably directed at the pitiful, whether our disposition to disgust is reliably directed toward the disgusting, whether we reliably fear the fearsome, or admire the admirable, without appealing to further emotions.

It is true that there are emotions we have learned not to trust very much (e.g., anger), and other emotions we have learned not to trust at all (e.g., envy), and by and large, our emotions tend to be exaggerated responses to situations. They are exaggerated in their range of generality (e.g., we fear the fearsome, but we also fear plenty of things that aren't fearsome), and they are exaggerated in their intensity. But it would be a mistake to think that suspicion of the exaggerated quality of emotion is grounds for a generalized mistrust of emotion. An exaggerated response can still be an exaggeration of the right response. We get too indignant, too disgusted, too fearful, too enthralled when in love, and so on, but it does not follow from *that* that emotions are inappropriate in the kind of response they are to their objects.

In any case, we have the same reason to trust our emotions as to trust our faculties of perception, memory, and reason. There are no noncircular grounds for believing they are reliable, but there *are* internal grounds for thinking that emotions that survive reflection are reliable. We trust what we think we see when we take a hard look in good environmental conditions, and if others agree, we take that as confirmation. Similarly, we trust what we feel when we feel admiration or pity or revulsion and continue to have the same emotion when we

---

[3] It is not usual to discuss the nature of emotion in a book of epistemology, but I will be discussing the epistemic importance of the emotion of admiration in this chapter. I have presented my general account of emotion in Zagzebski (2004a), Chapter Two.

reflect upon it later, and we take the agreement of others as confirmation. So we need to adopt a stance of basic trust in our epistemic faculties and emotions, at least we need to do so if we want to live a normal life.

Like everybody else, the conscientious believer trusts her faculties without evidence that they are reliable as a whole, but she learns through the use of her own faculties that she is not always reliable, and of course, she learns the same thing about other people. We all make mistakes, but we can learn from our mistakes by learning that many of our mistakes follow patterns. There are situations in which we are prone to perceptual errors, mistakes in memory, invalid forms of inference, influences of emotion that tend to inhibit the acquisition of true beliefs, and so on.

For example, sometimes we "see" what we expect to see and "hear" what we expect to hear.[4] When we repeatedly tell the story of an event, we become more sure of our recollections, so the more we retell a story, the more we convince ourselves that it is true, even if it is not.[5] Social psychologists have also discovered forms of bias such as the fundamental attribution error, the tendency for observers to underestimate the influence of the situation on the behavior of others and to overestimate the extent to which it expresses the individual's inner traits.[6] Many other patterns of error have been catalogued in books of formal and informal logic, and students often attempt to memorize these patterns in the hope that doing so will help them to improve their own ways of drawing inferences.

However, many patterns of error in our faculties are difficult to monitor in ourselves. In my opinion, it is harder to go through life consulting a long list of the patterns of behavior we should avoid than it is to acquire a few general traits of character that apply to a wide range of situations we encounter in our lives. I think this applies as much to the ethics of belief as to the ethics of action. Training the emotions is training what we do spontaneously. That is because emotions operate rapidly and tend to bypass cognitive function. By

---

[4] See Loftus (1996). The studies are supposed to show us something about perception, but they are actually studies of what people *remember* perceiving. These are cases of what is called the "misinformation effect."

[5] See Bregman and McAllister (1982) and Wells, Ferguson, and Lindsay (1981).

[6] Ross (1977) coined the phrase "fundamental attribution error." See also Allison, Mackie, Muller, and Worth (1993). Block and Funder (1986) claim that people of high social intelligence are more susceptible to the fundamental attribution error.

training our emotions in the right way, we become closer to the sort of person who automatically acts in the right way in many situations.

What I mean by a **virtue** is an acquired human excellence that includes a characteristic emotion disposition and reliable success at bringing about the end of the acts motivated by the emotion in question. Elsewhere (Zagzebski, 1996) I have applied this account of virtue to both moral and intellectual virtues. For example, I think that compassion is an acquired excellence that includes a characteristic disposition to feel compassion in certain circumstances (typically, circumstances in which one is faced with a suffering person), and reliable success in bringing about the end of acts motivated by compassion— roughly, alleviating the suffering. Fairness includes a characteristic disposition of impartiality toward other people in certain circumstances (such as distributing goods or burdens) and reliable success in bringing about a state of affairs that is the intended result of impartial treatment.

In this book we are interested in the intellectual virtues. These are the virtues that have as a component an emotion disposition that arises out of or depends upon the basic emotion of love of truth, or epistemic conscientiousness. In addition to a specific emotion disposition that arises from love of truth, I propose that each virtue of epistemic conscientiousness is such that its possession reliably succeeds at bringing about true beliefs through belief-forming acts motivated by the emotion characteristic of the virtue.

For example, open-mindedness is an acquired trait consisting of the disposition to be open to the views of others, even when they conflict with one's own views. This trait reliably leads to success in reaching the truth, other things being equal, through the cognitive behavior motivated by the emotion of openness to the views of others. So given two people who are otherwise alike except that one is open-minded and the other is not, the former's disposition of open-mindedness makes her more likely to get true beliefs than the latter. It is possible for a person to have the virtue of open-mindedness and not reliably get to the truth through cognitive behavior motivated by that emotion because of other features of her character or features of her environment. Nevertheless, open-mindedness is a trait the possession of which reliably leads a person to get the truth, other things being equal.[7] It is also possible for a person to get a true belief through open-minded behavior even though

---

[7] The comparative sense of "reliable" I am using here is not the one typically used by reliabilists. I am not claiming that most open-minded beliefs are true.

she does not have the virtue of open-mindedness because she does not have the general disposition of open-mindedness.

In this section we will focus on the subset of intellectual virtues that either restrain or enhance self-trust. When we train ourselves to be alert to new evidence, to be willing to criticize our own beliefs, and to be sensitive to the arguments of others, we learn to limit epistemic self-trust. It is significant that the virtues that limit or restrain self-trust presuppose that the agent is basically trustworthy. Intellectual attentiveness, carefulness, thoroughness, and openness to new evidence would not be virtues unless people were generally epistemically reliable. It would not do any good for a person to be attentive, thorough, and careful unless she was generally on the right track. If she is open to new evidence but is not trustworthy enough to know what to do with it, she is wasting her time.

I do not mean to say that the attentiveness or thoroughness of an otherwise untrustworthy person is not virtuous in that person.[8] But I do mean to say that part of the reason we consider attentiveness, thoroughness, and carefulness virtues is that we think they make it more likely that their possessors succeed in their end of reaching the truth, and these qualities would not do that unless, typically, the people who possess these qualities were already basically trustworthy. We assume the basic epistemic trustworthiness of human agents when we judge that the above qualities are intellectual virtues, and these traits are not virtues unless human agents are, in fact, generally trustworthy.

These virtues are rather vague, both in their domain of application and in the emotion dispositions and behavior dispositions that constitute the traits, so they need to be made more precise in order to be useful. Consider attentiveness. It can be crucially important to be attentive since inattentiveness can have tragic results, such as the conviction of an innocent person due to mistaken eyewitness testimony.[9]

---

[8] I discuss this issue in Zagzebski (1996), Part II, section 2.2. I argue that a virtue can make a person worse overall (e.g., the courageous Nazi), but even in such cases a virtue is worth having because it makes a person closer to the virtuous ideal. The courageous Nazi has less moral work to become a virtuous person than the cowardly Nazi. The former has to acquire justice and compassion. The latter has to acquire courage as well as justice and compassion.

[9] One analysis (Cutler and Penrod, 1995) estimates that 7,500 or 0.5% of 1.5 million American criminal convictions each year are in error, with roughly 4,500 of the errors due to mistaken identification. In Buckhout (1974), 141 students at California State University, Hayward, had witnessed an attack on a professor and were shown six pictures in order to identify the assailant. Sixty percent of the students identified an innocent man.

For that reason, jurors tend to think that a witness who can remember that there were three pictures on the wall must have been really paying attention, and they are more likely to believe the testimony of such a witness than one whose memory for trivial details is poor. But studies have shown that eyewitnesses with a poor memory for details tend to be the most *accurate* witnesses, whereas witnesses who notice details are less likely to pay attention to the culprit's face.[10]

Furthermore, some people can pay too much attention to sensory input with paralyzing results. Mark Haddon's delightful novel *The Curious Incident of the Dog in the Night-Time* (Doubleday, 2003) is about a fifteen-year-old boy with Asperger's Syndrome, a type of high-functioning autism. The boy is sometimes overwhelmed with sensory input, and to make it shut off, he closes his eyes and starts screaming. The data suggests, then, that what is important in acquiring the virtue of attentiveness is to be selectively attentive, to be attentive to the right thing, and that is much harder to define than the name "attentiveness" suggests.

In addition to acquiring virtues that limit epistemic self-trust, the conscientious believer attempts to avoid vices that are inappropriate forms of self-trust. These also are vaguely described in our common vocabulary and need to be made more precise to be useful in guiding our epistemic behavior. For instance, ordinary people routinely disparage so-called "wishful thinking," commonly defined as believing p out of a desire that p be true. But the situation is much more subtle than the name of the trait implies. For one thing, it is doubtful that it is psychologically possible to believe something solely because one wants it to be true, so on the above definition, wishful thinking may not even exist. Everyone wants to be good-looking, but how many people can get themselves to believe they are good-looking just because they want to believe it? The same point applies to wanting to be rich and famous, and more altruistic desires such as wanting peace and happiness in the world. What is more likely to happen is that a person weighs evidence for p differently than the evidence for *not-p* if she wants p to be true. That is common and interesting behavior, and it can be investigated empirically.

But if that is what wishful thinking is, it is not obviously a vice. Do we know that there is never a positive association between wanting p to be true and the truth of p? I have claimed several times

---

[10] See Wells and Leippe (1981) and Bell and Loftus (1989).

in this book that there is a natural belief that our faculties taken as a whole are truth-conducive, and I assume that we all want that to be true. I have also been at pains to argue that the belief is a reasonable one. There is probably a connection between the naturalness of the belief and its reasonableness, as well as a connection between the desire that the belief be true and its naturalness. I am not arguing that we have a right to believe that our faculties are reliable because we want to believe it, but it does seem to me that there is a nonaccidental connection between our desire and what is likely to be true in this case. We should not insist that any causal connection between desire and belief is an instance of the vice of wishful thinking. That does not mean that there is no such vice, but it does suggest that we should be careful to make the definition more precise.

In addition to virtues that limit epistemic self-trust, there are virtues that enhance it, such as intellectual courage, perseverance, and the virtue Roberts and Wood call "firmness," a trait they treat as an Aristotelian mean between intellectual flabbiness and rigidity (2007, ch. 7). Another way to look at this virtue is that it is the right degree of self-trust in the way we hold on to a belief. The intellectually firm agent has the appropriate degree of depth of assent in her beliefs. She is neither stubborn and unyielding and, hence, excessively trusting of herself, nor excessively pliable and wishy-washy and, hence, excessively mistrusting of herself.

Empirical research is helpful in making this virtue more precise also. There are studies that show that it is surprisingly difficult to overcome a false belief once a person acquires a rationale for it. In experiments in which a falsehood was planted in the minds of the subjects and later discredited, the belief survived intact in a very high percentage of cases.[11] There is also evidence that people tend to be overconfident in their beliefs, erring in the direction of what Roberts and Wood call rigidity.[12]

It is helpful to know the tendencies to error revealed in these studies. How should a conscientious believer react to them? In my experience, knowing about such studies automatically reduces a person's confidence in her judgments of the kind made in the studies, but the reaction is short-lived. We soon forget the mistakes to which we are prone, or we think that we are exceptional, more reasonable than

[11] See Ross and Anderson (1982).

[12] Kahneman and Tversky (1979).

the subjects in the studies. This latter response is an example of another tendency discovered in social psychology research: We tend to be overly positive in our appraisals of our own abilities and qualities.[13] All of this can make us rather disheartened about self-trust, but self-trust is not optional. It seems to me that the conscientious believer educates herself about tendencies to make mistakes that affect the formation of beliefs, and she then monitors her own behavior as well as she can. Even though we are not likely to detect every epistemic mistake we make, or even very many of them, knowing that we have made mistakes in the past and will no doubt continue to do so in the future fosters epistemic humility, a healthy trait for members of communities of virtually any kind.[14]

The intellectual virtues that enhance epistemic self-trust also presuppose one's general trustworthiness. We think that it is a good thing that an epistemic agent is courageous or persevering partly because we assume that the agent is more likely to get the truth with these traits than without them, but that assumption relies upon the further assumption that she is already generally epistemically trustworthy. An intellectually courageous unreliable person is not going to become any more reliable by being courageous, and similarly for the persevering believer. All of the virtues mentioned in this chapter so far presuppose the general trustworthiness of epistemic agents.

B. Trust in Admiration

What makes a trait an intellectual virtue? We might be tempted to think that a trait of intellectual character is virtuous because its possession is more truth-conducive than its lack, but I think that cannot be the full explanation for two reasons. One is that we treat traits like attentiveness, carefulness, thoroughness, intellectual courage, perseverance, and humility as prima facie virtues in advance of evidence of their truth-conduciveness. We assume that these traits are truth-conducive, under the assumption of general trustworthiness, but I doubt that we wait for that evidence before treating them as

---

[13] Myers (2005, p. 70) provides a list of domains in which people tend to demonstrate this self-serving bias, for example, in ethics, professional competence, virtue, intelligence, tolerance, and so on.

[14] See Chapter 9, "Humility," in Roberts and Wood (2007). See also their earlier paper, "Humility and Epistemic Goods," in DePaul and Zagzebski (2003).

virtues. The other reason is that we admire these traits more than we would if their goodness was limited to their truth-conduciveness.

Consider the way Alice Ambrose describes her experience of G. E. Moore as a teacher:

> Moore in his lectures was self-effacing. Criticisms he put forward of claims he himself had made, say in a previous lecture, could as well have been directed to an anonymous philosopher whose mistakes called for correction. For example, in discussing truth, Moore had examined the two propositional forms, "it is true that p" and "p," maintaining that they meant the same and therefore that "it is true that" has no meaning because "it is true that" is redundant. His comment in the next lecture: "My present view is that so far from its being the case that from the fact that it is redundant it follows that it has no meaning, it follows that if it is redundant *it has got meaning*. No phrase can be redundant in an expression without having a meaning." Some lectures later he notified his class: "I am going to make a jump now because I do not know how to go on."[15]

In discussing this passage, Roberts and Wood say that they do not see that "self-effacing" is the right word for Moore's behavior. He does not efface himself; he just pays little attention to himself because he has more important things to attend to. I agree with that. I find that I admire Moore as described by Ambrose, and continue to admire him upon reflection, and I trust that emotion. I might amend my judgment of Moore's admirability if I obtained evidence that his trait inhibited his intellectual pursuits in some way, or if I found out it was detrimental to his effectiveness as a teacher, so certain kinds of evidence could defeat my judgment of his admirability. My point is just that I do not make the judgment of his admirability because of evidence of the truth-conduciveness of the behavior, or any other evidence apart from the fact that I feel admiration for him and trust that emotion.

If you do not admire Moore as described by Ambrose, then you will make a different judgment about the virtuousness of the traits he exhibits, but I imagine that in that case, there will be certain other behaviors you admire in the intellectual realm, which would be the

---

[15] See Ambrose (1989). This passage is quoted in Roberts and Wood (2007, p. 240).

basis for other judgments about the content of the intellectual virtues. Either way, I think that trust in the emotion of admiration is the ground for the judgment that certain traits of character are virtuous and that certain traits of intellectual character are intellectually virtuous.

In Chapter One I argued that if we care about anything, we commit ourselves to caring about truth, and in this section I have argued that if we care about truth, we will be motivated to acquire other motives targeted to more specific epistemic circumstances or domains of knowing. So far I have focused on virtues that restrain or enhance epistemic self-trust, and I have argued that they are virtues only under the assumption that the agent is trustworthy, deserving of self-trust. Is self-trust itself a virtue? If we accept the Aristotelian view of virtue as an acquired trait, then under the assumption that self-trust is natural, it is not a virtue. However, self-trust when conjoined with the virtues that the conscientious believer acquires to restrain or enhance self-trust is virtuous. So conscientious self-trust is virtuous.

An important trait of self-trust that we have not yet investigated is intellectual autonomy. There are many different senses of autonomy, and I will make no attempt to investigate autonomy in all its significant forms, or in any detail in any of its forms. Instead, I want to focus on a form of intellectual autonomy that serves as the ideal for many philosophers, and I will argue in the next section that it cannot be supported. The failure of autonomy as an ideal is an important limitation on self-trust.

II. EPISTEMIC TRUST IN OTHERS AND THE VIRTUES OF EPISTEMIC COMMUNITIES

A. Epistemic Egoism as an Ideal

How should the conscientious believer treat the beliefs and faculties of other people? Of course, she trusts herself, but should she trust anybody else? Let's begin by distinguishing three positions regarding epistemic trust in others. As we will see, these positions are not exhaustive, but they are good focal points for discussion of trust and self-trust because all three of them have many adherents.

The first two positions are forms of **epistemic egoism**. The **extreme epistemic egoist** thinks that the fact that someone else believes *p* is never a reason for her to believe *p*, not even when conjoined with evidence that the other person is reliable. She will never believe on testimony. Before believing *p*, she will demand proof of *p* that she can determine by the use of her own faculties, given her own previous beliefs.

The **weak epistemic egoist** will treat the fact that someone else believes *p* as a reason for her to believe *p* provided that she has evidence that the other person is reliable. She will accept certain beliefs on testimony, but only when she has evidence that the testifier is trustworthy. So both kinds of egoist think that the fact that someone else has a certain belief is never *as such* a reason for them to believe it.[16]

We can call extreme antiegoism "epistemic universalism." The **epistemic universalist** always treats the fact that another person believes *p* as a reason to believe *p*, but that reason can be defeated by evidence of the person's unreliability or by evidence against *p*. For the universalist, then, the default position is to trust others. She needs a special reason not to trust them. For the weak egoist, the default position is to distrust others. She needs a special reason to trust them. The extreme egoist does not trust others, period.[17]

Many philosophers endorse some form of epistemic egoism under the name "**epistemic autonomy**." Elizabeth Fricker is a good example. She says: "This ideal type relies on no one else for any of her knowledge. Thus she takes no one else's word for anything, but accepts only what she has found out for herself, relying only on her own cognitive faculties and investigative and inferential powers."[18] This is a clear endorsement of what I have called extreme epistemic egoism. But Fricker goes on to observe that without reliance upon the testimony of others, we would not know or believe very much, so while she accepts extreme egoism as the ideal, she defends the weakening of the ideal in practice due to human limitations, endorsing a form of weak epistemic egoism.

---

[16] The argument of this section is taken from my paper "Ethical and Epistemic Egoism and the Ideal of Autonomy" (Zagzebski, 2007). In that paper I distinguish three degrees of epistemic egoism: extreme egoism, strong egoism, and weak egoism. In this book I find it less complicated to distinguish only two.

[17] I borrow the terms "epistemic egoism" and "epistemic universalism" from Richard Foley (2001), who endorses epistemic universalism.

[18] See Elizabeth Fricker (2006), p. 225, which can be found in Lackey and Sosa (2006).

Why would extreme epistemic egoism be an ideal? One answer might be that reliance upon the testimony of others makes us epistemically insecure, given that many people are untrustworthy. Fricker refers to this reason in explaining why a superior being would be able to live up to the ideal of extreme egoism:

> [A] superior being, with all the epistemic powers to find out everything she wanted to know for herself, could live up to this ideal of complete epistemic autonomy without thereby circumscribing the extent of her knowledge. Given the risks involved in epistemic dependence on others, . . . this superior being is, I suppose, epistemically better placed than humans are. That is, if she knew at first hand just as much as I myself know in large part through trust in others' testimony, she would be epistemically more secure, hence both practically more independent, and—in some abstract sense—more autonomous than I am. In the same way that I might regret that I cannot fly, or live to be 300 years old, I might regret that I am not such a being. (p. 243)

Fricker mentions the untrustworthiness of others as a reason for extreme egoism, although I doubt that she thinks it is the only reason. But does the untrustworthiness of others support extreme egoism? Why would I be any more secure if I rely only upon myself? Given that it is impossible for me to obtain evidence of my trustworthiness as a whole, it is impossible for me to have evidence that as a whole I am more trustworthy than other people. I have internal evidence, evidence using my powers, that many other people are untrustworthy, but I also have the same kind of evidence that I am sometimes untrustworthy, and I have evidence that in some domains some other people are more trustworthy than I am.

As far as I can see, fear of untrustworthiness can make us epistemically insecure, but it does not support extreme epistemic egoism. Furthermore, if the untrustworthiness of others is the ground of the ideal of extreme egoism, that does not explain why the ideal is not one in which persons are epistemically dependent upon perfectly trustworthy other persons. It is doubtful, then, that if extreme epistemic egoism is an ideal, it is because of the epistemic untrustworthiness of others.

Considerations on the ethics of belief that we discussed in Chapter One might give us another reason for embracing extreme epistemic egoism. One of the morals of Clifford's example of the ship owner is that we are morally responsible for our beliefs, at least those beliefs that lead to action. It could be argued that if we believe on the testimony of others, we are illegitimately shifting responsibility for our beliefs to somebody else. If we cannot take the trouble to think for ourselves, we cannot take the trouble to be morally responsible agents. But we are blameworthy for our morally wrong acts no matter where we get the beliefs upon which the acts are based, so we had better not rely upon testimony for those beliefs.

As far as I can see, this argument will not work either. In Chapter One I argued that both the degree of the requirement to be conscientious and the degree of the conscientiousness demanded varies with the importance of the domain of belief in question, which means that when something morally significant is at stake, there is a strong moral demand on us to be very conscientious in our belief. So there is a strong demand on the ship owner to be very conscientious in his belief that his ship is seaworthy. That means the ship owner must care about the truth in this particular case very much and act epistemically in a way appropriate to that degree of caring. But is there any reason to think that the more conscientious he is, the less he will rely upon testimony? When something morally important is at stake, the moral demand on him is to *try hard to get a true belief.* It would not follow that he should rely only upon his own belief-forming processes and not those of others unless he has reason to think that he is more trustworthy than others, and we have already seen that he does not in general have reason to think that. In fact, in the ship owner case, the situation is quite the reverse. In that case, conscientiousness places a demand on the ship owner to seek the testimony of the relevant experts.

What about weak egoism? Would the conscientious believer always demand evidence of the reliability of another before taking the other's word for something morally important? Only if love of truth requires the adoption of the default position of trust in self combined with distrust of others. If the conscientious believer thinks that in the absence of evidence he should trust himself more than somebody else whose reliability is undetermined, then he will be a weak egoist, but what would be his grounds for such a position? Whatever they are, it is not conscientiousness that leads him to be a weak egoist.

Caring about truth does mean that it is irresponsible to be epistemically lazy. I assume that passively accepting the views of others when one is capable of critically evaluating those views oneself is epistemically vicious, but I do not see any reason to think that the conscientious believer would be an egoist. If there is a defense for egoism, it does not come from the requirements of conscientiousness, so the second argument does not support epistemic egoism.

I suspect that the real reason many people think of epistemic egoism as an ideal is that they admire the perfectly independent thinker, and they trust their admiration. Who could fail to be moved by Ralph Waldo Emerson's classic essay "Self-Reliance," in which he describes the romantic attraction of the autonomous thinker in vivid prose?

> The magnetism which all original action exerts is explained when we inquire the reason of self-trust. Who is the trustee? What is the aboriginal self, on which a universal reliance may be grounded? What is the nature and power of that science-baffling star, without parallax, without calculable elements, which shoots a ray of beauty even into trivial and impure actions, if the least mark of independence appear? (Emerson 1968, p. 98)

Earlier Emerson says, "[T]he highest merit we ascribe to Moses, Plato, and Milton is that they set at naught books and traditions, and spoke not what men, but what *they* thought" (p. 89). According to Emerson, the admirability of the self-reliant person has nothing to do with his confidence in his trustworthiness: "I remember an answer which when quite young I was prompted to make to a valued adviser who was wont to importune me with the dear old doctrines of the church. On my saying, 'What have I to do with the sacredness of traditions, if I live wholly from within?' my friend suggested—'But these impulses may be from below, not from above.' I replied, 'They do not seem to me to be such; but if I am the Devil's child, I will live then from the Devil' " (p. 92).

Since I have said that it is reasonable to trust our emotion of admiration when it is reflective and shared by trusted others, I will not argue against the admirability of the extreme egoist. Perhaps that issue could be resolved if we were able to look at extended narratives in which the extreme egoist is compared with other intellectual types. I do not know of any narratives of that kind, but I think they would be helpful. Even then, I suspect that the issue would not be resolved. There are no doubt deep and irresolvable conflicts of emotion between people, just as there are deep and irresolvable conflicts of belief, the topic of the next section, so we may not be able to agree on the admirability of the extreme egoist by this approach.

My own view is that what is admirable about Moses, Plato, and Milton is something other than epistemic egoism—their creative genius, originality, and distinctive personal and intellectual powers.[19] But I will not try to convince anybody that the extreme egoist is not admirable. Instead, I will argue that neither form of epistemic egoism is a coherent position to take. Conscientiousness requires the agent to reject epistemic egoism.

B. The Incoherence of Epistemic Egoism

If the egoist cares about anything, then, like everybody else, she is committed to being a conscientious believer; she is committed to caring about the truth. I interpret the epistemic egoist as somebody who *does* care about the truth. What makes her an epistemic egoist is that she trusts herself more than others to get the truth. It is rational for the egoist to trust herself when she is conscientious. She also has evidence that she gets the truth when she is conscientious, but like everybody else, she must trust herself in advance of the evidence. So the rational epistemic egoist trusts herself when she is conscientious in attempting to get the truth, and this trust is not based on evidence of her trustworthiness.

But if the epistemic egoist is rational, she is committed to trusting others when they are conscientious, when they exhibit the behaviors she trusts in herself. Trusting herself commits her to trusting others when they are in the same position she is in; that is, when they are in similar circumstances, have apparently similar powers and abilities, and act as conscientiously as she acts when she trusts herself. If she is consistent, she must trust them as much as herself, other things being equal, since she has no basis upon which to trust herself more than those she perceives to be epistemically equally well-placed.

Let me stress that my point is not that she is committed to trusting them because she has evidence that they are trustworthy. She is committed to trusting them because there is no relevant difference between her grounds for trusting herself and her grounds for trusting them. Assuming it is reasonable to trust herself, it is reasonable to trust others. If she insists upon trusting herself—her faculties,

---

[19] We might associate their intellectual power with autonomy because of a deeper view about perfection. Traditionally, God has the attribute of aseity, an extreme independence from creatures that Aquinas interpreted as requiring God to know everything through his knowledge of himself. If God is an extreme epistemic egoist, we might think of extreme egoism as a virtue in creatures as well. I thank Eric Yang for this point.

beliefs, and emotions—more than others, she must be trusting her faculties, beliefs, and emotions just because they are her own and not someone else's. She cannot consistently do that if she thinks there is any reason to trust herself. Any reason she can point to is a reason that applies to many others.

There is the possibility that she trusts herself without any reason at all and distrusts others without any reason at all. She could be a person who cares about her own powers and beliefs just because they are hers, who cares about her own powers and beliefs more than the truth. In that case, she is not an epistemic egoist; she is an extreme ethical egoist in the realm of the intellect. Unlike epistemic egoism, ethical egoism has very few defenders. I think, then, that unless she wants to adopt such an unappealing position, she is forced to reject both extreme and weak epistemic egoism.

It follows that if epistemic autonomy is interpreted as one of the forms of egoism I have described, then epistemic autonomy is an incoherent ideal. It is not sensible to have a desire for truth and to trust my own faculties that generate and support my beliefs, but reject trust in the faculties of others.

Perhaps some other form of epistemic autonomy survives. Roberts and Wood defend a virtue they call intellectual autonomy "according to which one becomes an integrated, independent thinker by fittingly appropriating one's vast intellectual debts and dependencies" (Roberts and Wood, 2007, p. 257). As they characterize autonomy, it is a more subtle and complex trait than mere intellectual independence, although it includes a measure of independence as a component. Roberts and Wood suggest that perhaps the desire to be independent is natural (p. 281). I find that an interesting suggestion, one that might explain the admiration many people feel for the autonomous intellect. In any case, I think that the concept of autonomy is as important in epistemology as in ethics, and it deserves much more investigation than we have seen up to now.

Notice that the rejection of epistemic egoism does not commit us to epistemic universalism. Epistemic egoism is the position that the fact that someone else believes p is never as such a reason to believe p oneself. Even the weak egoist maintains that the fact that someone else believes p must be conjoined with evidence of the believer's reliability before giving me *any* reason to believe p. Epistemic universalism is the position that the fact that someone else believes p is *always* a reason for believing p oneself, even though that reason can be defeated by other evidence. The rejection of egoism does not entail universalism. Middle positions are possible, and we will turn to such a position in the next section.

If I am right in my argument that the logic of self-trust requires us to place epistemic trust in some other people, then we must treat the beliefs of at least some other people as relevant to the reasonable formation and maintenance of our own beliefs. I think there are intellectual virtues that enhance epistemic trust in others, just as there are virtues that enhance epistemic self-trust, and there are virtues that restrain epistemic trust in others, just as there are virtues that restrain self-trust.[20] For instance, I think that open-mindedness, intellectual humility, and intellectual tolerance are traits that enhance trust in others, and these traits would not be virtues unless basic trust in others was justified. If others were not basically trustworthy, their opinions would be irrelevant to the beliefs of reasonable people, and there would be no reason to listen to their views open-mindedly or humbly. Even epistemic fairness may presuppose a baseline of minimal trustworthiness among all people, although I am less sure about that virtue.[21]

In the last section I made the parallel point about self-trust. There are virtues that restrain or enhance self-trust that would not be virtues unless the self is basically trustworthy, and there are virtues that restrain or enhance trust in others that would not be virtues unless others are basically trustworthy.

Notice that if we accept either form of egoism, the virtues that enhance trust in others are not virtues. The extreme egoist would not be open to consideration of the views of others, and the weak egoist

---

[20] The virtues that enhance or restrain self-trust are not necessarily distinct from virtues that enhance or restrain trust in others. For instance, open-mindedness and intellectual humility both restrain self-trust and enhance trust in others. Intellectual courage both enhances self-trust and restrains trust in others.

[21] Some virtues in the intellectual realm are not intellectual virtues in the sense I have described because they do not involve motives that pertain to the intellect. Instead, they are moral virtues applied to the intellectual realm. Moral fairness involves a characteristic attitude or emotion of respect toward others that leads to treating them in the way we call fair, however that is defined. Moral fairness no doubt applies to the way we treat their beliefs, among other things. So even though moral fairness applies in the intellectual realm, it arises from emotion dispositions directed toward other persons. I distinguish that kind of virtue from one that arises from love of truth or other epistemic goods. It would be interesting to pursue the issue of whether intellectual fairness is an intellectual virtue arising from epistemic conscientiousness or the disposition to care about some other intellectual good, or whether instead intellectual fairness is nothing more than moral fairness applied to the opinions of others.

would be open to their views only when she has evidence that they are reliable. If the weak egoist listens to the views of others, it is because the use of her own faculties shows her that they are reliable, and she listens to them only because of that evidence, not because of motives of open-mindedness or intellectual humility. The epistemic egoist treats the views of others as unworthy of attention in themselves, even though the weak egoist treats them as worthy of attention when the evidence points to the reliability of the source. There is no reason for the egoist to think that a disposition to pay attention to others is virtuous except insofar as it is dictated by the injunction to follow the evidence. It is not virtuous to trust others in advance of the evidence. The epistemic egoist will not necessarily be intellectually arrogant or vain, but if the egoist thinks that humility is superior to vanity or arrogance, it is because she thinks acting humbly is dictated by the injunction to weigh the evidence, not because of the recognition of the admirability of the trait of humility. Presumably, then, the egoist would say that Moore as described by Ambrose is virtuous only if and to the extent to which his humble behavior makes him reliable. The egoist does not trust her emotion of admiration in the way she trusts her other basic faculties.

C. Virtues of Epistemic Communities

So far we have discussed only virtues that produce and regulate our own beliefs, but if we have both self-trust and trust in others, we become members of epistemic communities, the purpose of which is not limited to our personal search for truth. If we are lovers of truth, we are motivated to be purveyors of truth to others. Since a conscientious person cares that others have the truth too, she is not epistemically stingy, and she tries to acquire traits that make her a credible informant to other people. In Chapter One we discussed the tragedy of Cassandra, who was cursed by Zeus to be disbelieved by the members of her epistemic community. In her case it was not her fault that nobody believed her, but many times our lack of credibility is due to personal failings that prevent us from being good informers or teachers. Virtues of good pedagogy like clarity and convincingness require both a good grasp of what one tells others, as well as confidence in oneself. Some of these virtues limit and balance the virtues of trust in others such as open-mindedness and humility.

Epistemic generosity is another virtue of the conscientious member of an epistemic community. Generosity in the ordinary moral sense is usually thought to involve giving a good to someone else at one's own expense. If I give you money, I have less myself. If I give you my time, I have less time to spend on something else. Epistemic generosity is primarily the giving of knowledge. If I give you some of my knowledge, I do not lose the knowledge myself, and can even gain knowledge in the process of giving it to you. So it might seem strange to think of giving knowledge as requiring generosity. Yet I think that experience shows that there are people who are much more willing to share their knowledge and expertise than are others. Even though giving away knowledge does not take away the teacher's own knowledge, it reduces the difference between the teacher's level of knowledge and the student's, and once the student learns how to learn, the student may even come to surpass the teacher. If we care more about our own status than conveying knowledge to others, we become epistemically stingy. If generosity is the virtue opposed to stinginess, I think that means that conscientious members of epistemic communities need to be epistemically generous.[22]

There are no doubt many other virtues of members of epistemic communities, such as epistemic fairness and tolerance. There may also be virtues that inhere in communities themselves rather than in individuals. An examination of epistemic justice would be interesting because it could turn out that an epistemically virtuous community needs structures for the practices of epistemic praise and blame, designed to inhibit bullshit, lying, and other attacks on the value of truth.[23] There are probably also virtues that we want some but not all members of a community to have. I suspect that intellectual originality is in this category. We would not want everybody to be a Plato or a Milton, but we are better off as a community with the occasional brilliant and original mind.

I hope that epistemologists in the future will do much more investigation on the nature and purpose of epistemic communities. Moral philosophers investigate moral communities and such communal goods as peace, justice, and welfare. Arguably, these goods are not limited to divisible goods—goods that are exhaustively divided among individuals, but involve goods that are possessed by the community itself. It is a task for moral philosophy to investigate the conditions that produce these goods and the virtues that permit

[22] For a discussion of intellectual generosity, see Roberts and Wood (2007), Chapter 11.

[23] For more on epistemic justice, see Miranda Fricker (2007).

TRUST AND THE INTELLECTUAL VIRTUES

the community to possess them in a robust sense. Similarly, it seems to me that the goods of epistemic communities might not all be divisible. Epistemic justice and epistemic welfare are closely parallel to justice and welfare in the moral sense, and may also be nondivisible. In any case, we need to see a lot more work on the conditions that produce and maintain epistemic communities that have the goods we desire.

III. IRRESOLVABLE EPISTEMIC DISAGREEMENT

An important legacy of John Locke and other Enlightenment thinkers is *intellectual egalitarianism*.[24] The idea is that all normal human beings are roughly equal in their capacity to get knowledge. Aside from the fact that some have acquired greater expertise or have greater access to information in some fields, there are no epistemic elites. A belief in intellectual egalitarianism is deeply embedded in contemporary Western culture, probably because it is associated with democracy, but I am interested in it here because it can be used to support *epistemic universalism*, the third position on trust in others mentioned at the beginning of the last section.[25] The epistemic universalist always treats the fact that another person believes *p* as a prima facie reason to believe *p* herself. Belief that *p* can be defeated, and perhaps it even can be defeated rather quickly, but what makes a person a universalist is that she places prima facie epistemic trust in every other person, treating all persons in the world at all times as equally trustworthy prior to obtaining evidence of the greater trustworthiness of some over others.

I find it hard to know if I am a universalist because there are no pure test cases in which I know literally nothing at all about a person

---

[24] Foley brings up this "Lockean presupposition," along with Locke's other two presuppositions, optimism and individualism, in Foley (2001), pp. 89–92.

[25] Foley (2001) uses egalitarianism in his defense of epistemic universalism. I interpret Foley's version of epistemic universalism as stronger than the one I mention above. He argues that it is reasonable to adopt a belief *p* based solely on the fact that somebody else believes *p* until it is defeated by further evidence. The form of universalism I give here is the position that the fact that someone else believes *p* always gives me *a* reason in favor of believing *p*. See Foley (2001), Chapter 4, esp. pp. 89–92 and 122–25.

except that he or she believes *p*, and where I neither believe nor disbelieve *p* in advance, I have no evidence for or against *p*, and believing *p* does not affect anything else I trust in myself. However, I think we can make up test cases that are fairly close to pure cases, and I have found that people differ in their responses to them.

Here is a case you can use to test your intuitions about universalism. Suppose that you know very little about medieval Poland or the Tartars, but you find out that somebody of whom you know nothing believes that Poland was invaded by the Tartars in 1241. Suppose also that if you adopted that belief, it would not affect anything else you trust, whether a belief, an emotion, or a past memory. I'll leave it to the reader to fill in the details about how you find out that somebody has this belief. Maybe you overhear it in someone's conversation, or you read it on Wikipedia. In either of those cases, of course, you would know *something* about the source, but try to forget that information. The issue then is this: Would you count the fact that somebody believes that Poland was invaded by the Tartars in 1241 as a reason to believe it yourself? The universalist says yes. In the absence of evidence, the epistemic universalist treats the fact that someone else believes *p* as a reason for her to believe *p*.

Now if you are an epistemic egalitarian and universalist, you get a problem in resolving conflict in the beliefs of two persons, even when one of those persons is yourself. Of course, many conflicts can be resolved on the basis of evidence, but many cannot be. What should a reasonable person do? Suppose the conflict is between her own belief and that of another. If she favors her own belief just because it is hers, isn't she assuming, unjustifiably, that she is more trustworthy than the other person? And if she adopts the other person's belief, she will be unjustifiably assuming that he is more trustworthy than she is. Neither believer has a sufficient epistemic reason to maintain his or her belief, and neither believer has a reason to switch his or her position, since the believer will then be in the same position from which he or she started. Let us call this the Enlightenment Worry: *Irresolvable disagreement over a belief threatens the conscientiousness of the belief.* This worry is a problem for many of our beliefs, including religious, moral, and political beliefs that we may cherish.

It may be tempting to think that we can escape the Enlightenment Worry by rejecting epistemic universalism and egalitarianism. How many of us feel threatened by disagreements with people whom we do not admire? If you believe acts of terrorism or genocide are wrong (by whatever definition you want), I doubt that you think the conscientiousness of your belief is threatened when you find out there are people who disagree, even though you are not likely to resolve the conflict by talking it over with them with all the evidence in hand. If you think that it is a bad idea to devote your life primarily to acquiring money and fame, I doubt that it will bother you to find out that there are people who think the contrary. Nor should it.

But if we escape the Enlightenment Worry on the grounds that a conscientious person's beliefs are not threatened by the beliefs of persons she does not admire, we run immediately into another version of the worry. We recognize admirable people among those who believe differently than we do, and we observe that the beliefs of different exemplars conflict with each other. There are people who are admirable both intellectually and morally. They have all the virtues a conscientious person tries to acquire, and they are intelligent and informed. They have whatever we find epistemically trustworthy in other persons in a superlative degree. But they sometimes disagree with us in a way that cannot be resolved. Furthermore, they disagree with each other. If you are like me and trust your emotion of admiration more than you trust egalitarianism, you will find the problem of irresolvable disagreement among people you admire and between those people and yourself a more threatening problem than the Enlightenment Worry.

Notice that as I have posed the problem of disagreement, the conflict is not simply a conflict between self-trust and trust in others; it is a conflict within self-trust. That is because self-trust includes trust in the emotions we have upon reflection. To trust an emotion means to have confidence that the emotion is appropriate for the circumstances. To trust one's emotion of admiration is to trust that those we admire (upon reflection, and with agreement from others whom we trust) are, in fact, admirable. The way I understand the admirable, it is something like the imitably attractive. We feel a positive emotion toward the person we admire that would lead to imitating the person, given the right practical conditions. So to trust the emotion of admiration means to have confidence that it is appropriate to feel the kind of attraction and desire to imitate that is intrinsic to admiration. If a person whom I admire and the admirability of whom I trust has a belief that conflicts with one of my own beliefs, a belief that I trust, there is a conflict within my trust in myself.

To solve the problem, I think we need to delve more deeply into the implications of self-trust. In some cases I can resolve the conflict by asking myself, "What do I trust more, my admiration of this person, or my belief?" Suppose that it is the former. I trust my admiration, so I trust that the person is admirable, and thus worthy of imitation, more than I trust that my belief is true. Maybe I do not admire the way I formed my own belief as much as I admire the way the other person formed his. Suppose also that I am not aware of another person I admire just as much whose belief agrees with mine. Self-trust would lead me to trust the admired person's belief more than my own. If I am able to imitate the admired person by adopting his belief without changing anything else about myself that I trust even more than I trust my admiration for him, then self-trust should lead me to change my belief.

I think this is the right way to proceed if the belief in question is not deeply embedded in the self, say, a belief about the best brand of audio equipment. It might seem to be a trivial point to say that we are committed by self-trust to change beliefs that are relatively trivial, but I don't think it is trivial at all. Most of our beliefs are in this category, and it is significant if we commit ourselves to changing them when we trust our admiration for a person with an opposing belief more than our belief.

But even if I trust my admiration for another person more than I trust my belief, it does not always follow that I should change it. Whether I should change a belief is not simply determined by how much I trust the belief, but by how much I trust the other aspects of myself that I would have to change if I changed the belief. Given the social construction of many of our beliefs, trusting those beliefs commits us to trusting the traditions that shape us and the institutions on which we depend.

Religious and moral beliefs are usually connected with a network of other beliefs, and many of those beliefs are connected with emotions, experiences, and communal loyalties, all of which we may trust. So I might trust my admiration for a Hindu, and in particular, I might trust my admiration for the way the Hindu believes p more than I trust my own belief not-p, but I might not trust the way the Hindu believes p as much as I trust some of the other beliefs, emotions, and communal loyalties that I would have to change if I imitated the Hindu by believing p myself. So I can admire the belief system of a Hindu without the inclination to adopt that system for myself, and that can be a conscientious response.

Suppose, however, that I trust my admiration for the Hindu more than I trust the aspects of myself I would have to change if I imitated the Hindu by adopting his religion. In that case, the conscientious thing to do might be to convert to Hinduism. I am not aware of many philosophers who investigate the epistemological issues raised by the phenomenon of conversion, but I think that the rationality of radical and wholesale belief change is very interesting. One of the things I trust is my belief that there are people who are reasonable in making radical changes in their beliefs. Religious heroes of history are often people who make an abrupt change with their past at some point in their lives, and from that time onward their beliefs change dramatically. What would make that reasonable? It certainly isn't their evidence, which changes little or not at all from their preconversion epistemic state. The most obvious change is probably in their emotions, and that affects the reasonableness of their beliefs only if emotion can affect the reasonableness of beliefs, as I have argued it does.

But I also trust my belief that most of the time, it is not reasonable to make radical changes in our beliefs. Radical conversion is not only unusual in its rate of occurrence, but also unusual in its reasonableness. I do not see any way to explain that without focusing on the reasonableness of self-trust and the fact that we trust some aspects of ourselves more than others, and are reasonable in doing so. Ultimately, there is something in the self that is the final authority. We may admire alternate ways of life and the beliefs that go with them and trust that admiration. At the same time, we may have full confidence in the beliefs, emotions, and their sources in the traditions that shape us, and I think most of us are conscientious in doing so.

The conflict within self-trust that arises from irresolvable conflict in belief between ourselves and people we admire forces us to put those aspects of ourselves we trust the most in the forefront of our consciousness. The challenge of doing that is probably good for us, but I don't think we have any rule for determining the way to do it conscientiously. You might trust certain aspects of yourself more than your urge to imitate an admired person, but how can you tell that you *should* do that? The evidence does not determine what you should do, and self-trust in itself does not determine what you should do since the conflict arises within self-trust.

I suspect that this problem cannot be solved without an investigation of the nature of the self. This is one of the points at which epistemology leaves off and another important field of philosophy begins, so I will drop the issue, but I hope that interested students will think about the connection between the nature of the self and the important issue of how to resolve conflicts within our beliefs and between our beliefs and other aspects of the self.[26]

IV. SUMMARY

In this chapter I have argued that epistemic conscientiousness motivates an epistemic agent to acquire a large number of intellectual virtues that are connected to self-trust and trust in others in important ways. I have also argued that trust in others is entailed by self-trust, and that epistemic egoism is incoherent. Since epistemic autonomy is often understood in a way that makes it indistinguishable from epistemic egoism, it follows that epistemic autonomy as commonly understood is incoherent. It is not a virtue.

Since the arguments of this chapter involve a sequence of interconnected points, continuing points made in Chapters One and Three, it might be helpful to summarize the whole chapter, including the points I am using from other chapters.

(1) In Chapter One I argued that if we care about anything, we commit ourselves to caring about truth in the domains we care about. That is, we commit ourselves to being epistemically conscientious in those domains. Given that there are some domains about which caring is not optional, the range of beliefs that must be epistemically conscientious is probably very wide. It might not include all of our beliefs, but it certainly includes a substantial proportion of them.

(2) We cannot have noncircular evidence that our faculties taken as a whole reliably get us to the truth, so to live a normal life, we need basic epistemic self-trust. Basic self-trust includes trust in our perceptual and cognitive faculties, and in some emotions such as admiration. It is reasonable for all human beings to have basic self-trust.

(3) The conscientious person has internal (circular) evidence that she makes mistakes, and she learns from that evidence to monitor her epistemic behavior. She avoids patterns of belief-formation she

---

[26] The argument of this section is taken in part from Zagzebski (2006a), reprinted in *Liberal Faith: Essays in Honor of Philip Quinn*, edited by Paul Weithman, forthcoming, University of Notre Dame Press, 2008.

discovers to be unreliable, and she attempts to acquire traits of intellectual character that she admires epistemically. These are the intellectual virtues. They include attentiveness, intellectual carefulness, thoroughness, courage, perseverance, firmness, humility, generosity, and open-mindedness.

(4) These intellectual virtues restrain or enhance self-trust or trust in others. The traits that restrain or enhance self-trust would not be virtues unless the self is trustworthy. The traits that restrain or enhance trust in others would not be virtues unless others are trustworthy. Under the assumption that people are basically trustworthy, these traits aid an epistemic agent in obtaining true beliefs. An agent has conscientious self-trust when she has these qualities.

(5) The epistemic egoist trusts herself, but (in different degrees discussed above) does not trust others. However, since the egoist commits herself to caring about truth and trusts herself when she is conscientious, she is committed to trusting others when they are conscientious, that is, when they exhibit the traits and behaviors she trusts in herself. Epistemic autonomy in the sense of any degree of epistemic egoism addressed in this chapter is not a virtue. In fact, it is an inconsistent ideal.

(6) The epistemically conscientious person would have no reason to acquire some of the intellectual virtues if epistemic egoism were correct. The conscientious person would not have a reason to acquire traits like epistemic humility, tolerance, and open-mindedness unless she trusts others in a sense that requires the rejection of egoism. That is, the conscientious person is motivated to acquire these traits only if she is not an epistemic egoist. (This is a different point than point 4, that these traits are virtues only if other people are trustworthy.)

Almost all of the virtues discussed in this chapter are traits that restrain or enhance self-trust or trust in others, and they presuppose the basic trustworthiness of ourselves and others. There are probably some intellectual virtues, traits that we admire intellectually, that are not in this category. I briefly mentioned intellectual originality and creativity, and I think those are examples of virtues that are not related to trust or trustworthiness in the ways I have described in this chapter.

Nothing I have said so far relates conscientiousness or the intellectual virtues to knowledge. I think that the connection between the intellectual virtues and caring about truth, and between the intellectual virtues and self-trust, gives us a sufficient reason to take the intellectual virtues seriously in our epistemic lives. However, I will argue in the next chapter that there is another important reason to give the intellectual virtues a central place in epistemology: I think that they are directly related to the nature of knowledge.

FURTHER READING

In addition to my book *Virtues of the Mind* (Cambridge: Cambridge University Press, 1996), I have co-edited two volumes of papers related to virtue epistemology. Michael DePaul and Linda Zagzebski (eds.), *Intellectual Virtue: Perspectives from Ethics and Epistemology* (Oxford: Clarendon Press, 2003) includes essays by both virtue ethicists and virtue epistemologists on virtue-theoretic approaches to knowledge, epistemic values, understanding, and humility. Abrol Fairweather and Linda Zagzebski, *Virtue Epistemology: Essays on Epistemic Virtue and Responsibility* (Oxford: Oxford University Press, 2001) contains essays by both virtue epistemologists and traditional epistemologists. I have mentioned several times in this chapter the very interesting book by Robert C. Roberts and Jay W. Wood, *Intellectual Virtues: An Essay in Regulative Epistemology* (Oxford: Oxford University Press, 2007). For a different approach to virtue epistemology, see Ernest Sosa's *A Virtue Epistemology: Apt Belief and Reflective Knowledge* (Oxford: Oxford University Press, 2007). Finally, the advanced reader interested in self-trust and trust in others may consult Keith Lehrer, *Self-Trust: A Study of Reason, Knowledge, and Autonomy* (Oxford: Oxford University Press, 1997), and Richard Foley, *Intellectual Trust in Oneself and Others* (Cambridge: Cambridge University Press, 2001).

5

What Is Knowledge?

I. INTRODUCTION

At the beginning of Chapter One we considered three central questions in epistemology: What is knowledge? Is knowledge possible? How do we get knowledge? In Chapters Two and Three we examined the second question, and in Chapter Four I began a nonconventional approach to the third. We now turn to the first question. At the end of this chapter we will return to the third.

The question we are now investigating could be more accurately phrased as "What is knowing?" rather than "What is knowledge?" Although the word "knowledge" often refers to the state of knowing, it can also be used to refer to the objects of states of knowing, as when we speak of "a body of knowledge." Our interest in this chapter is knowledge in the first sense. What does it take for a person like you or me to know something?

Here are a few of the proposed definitions of knowledge (knowing) we have encountered so far in this book:

(i) Knowledge is justified true belief.

(ii) Knowledge is true belief arising from a reliable belief-forming process.

(iii) Knowledge is true belief supported by evidence that eliminates all possibilities except those we are properly ignoring.

These three definitions have a common pattern identified in Chapter One: Knowledge is true belief + x, where x is a good way to believe. Since presumably believing the truth is good anyway,[1] x must be something that makes true believing even better.

Much of this chapter will be devoted to identifying the x feature and its constraints on the way we define knowledge. I will then propose a general schema for defining knowledge and will proceed to make it more specific. But before we get to that, let us review the components of knowledge that are *not* the focus of contemporary debates.

Most epistemologists take for granted that knowing is a species of believing. If I know *p*, then I believe *p*. This point deserves some comment because occasionally in the history of philosophy belief and knowledge were regarded as mutually exclusive states, either because it was thought that knowledge and belief have distinct objects, or because it was thought appropriate to restrict the range of belief to epistemic states evaluatively inferior to the state of knowing. Plato referred to both reasons for his view that knowledge (*epistêmê*) and belief (*doxa*) are mutually exclusive.[2] The first worry has been resolved to the satisfaction of most contemporary philosophers by the adoption of the view that propositions are the objects of belief as well as of knowledge, and, in fact, the same proposition can be either known or believed. So a person may know today what he only believed yesterday—say, that his favorite team would win the game today. As we saw in Chapter One, however, some knowledge is nonpropositional, but as long as we restrict the discussion to propositional knowledge, there should be no objection to the idea that knowledge is a form of belief on the grounds of a difference in their objects.

The second worry is settled if we adopt another convention mentioned in Chapter One, the stipulation that to believe is to *think with assent*, a definition that comes from Augustine. Since it is indisputable that to know propositionally is (among other things) to take a proposition to be true, and if to assent to a proposition just *is* to take it to be true, then on the Augustinian definition of belief it follows that knowing is a form of believing. Of course, there is nothing to stop someone from making a different stipulation, for example, that believing is assenting to a true proposition in a way inferior to knowing, in

---

[1] We will examine whether and how true belief is good in Chapter Six.

[2] See particularly the line analogy in the *Republic* 509d–511e, and the famous Allegory of the Cave 514a–518d.

which case believing and knowing would be mutually exclusive. But even if we adopt that convention, it is plain that believing and knowing have something in common, and we need a term for that. If believing is not thinking with assent, then something else is, in which case knowing is a form of that something else. For the sake of convenience, I will continue to follow the convention of calling it "believing."

Even though it is reasonable to maintain that knowing is a form of believing, that may not be helpful to a quest for a definition of knowledge since belief is in need of definition also. Some philosophers maintain that knowledge is the more basic concept,[3] and some argue that the concept of belief has outlived its usefulness and should be eliminated.[4] Still, epistemologists commonly think that knowing is the more complex state; it involves *at least* thinking with assent. So if we say knowing is thinking with assent plus x, then we are part way toward identifying the components of knowledge. Identifying the main components of something is one way of defining it. It is not the only way, but I think it will turn out to be a helpful one in this case.

Another relatively uncontroversial feature of knowledge is that its object is a *true* proposition. The attempt to get knowledge is the attempt to figure out what the truth is about the world. If we think hard and come to believe something false, then no matter how conscientious we are, our belief cannot be knowledge because we failed in our attempt to get the truth. Knowledge implies success in reaching our epistemic end and the basic epistemic end is truth. The further question, "What is truth?," is generally treated outside epistemology, so I will not say anything more about it, but obviously the answer to that question bears on the question for this chapter in an important way.

So knowledge is at least true belief, or believing a true proposition, but rarely have philosophers thought that true belief is sufficient for knowledge.[5] There are at least two types of cases of true believing that fail to reach the level of knowing. One is the case of getting a true belief completely by luck, for example, by a lucky guess. You might guess that the number of cars in the parking lot is 167 and have the urge to believe your own guess, but even if the guess is correct,

<hr>

[3] See Williamson (2000) and Hawthorne (2004). Their reasoning has to do, in part, with comparing knowledge and action.

[4] See Stich (1983) and (1990). Other eliminativist strategies can be found in Dennett (1987) and Churchland (1988).

[5] For an exception to the view that knowledge is a better or different state than true belief, see Sartwell (1992) and Hetherington (2001).

surely you do not know that there are 167 cars in the lot.[6] The second type of case is the unconscientious true belief. I think that most persons who reflect upon Clifford's ship owner agree that the ship owner did not know that his ship was seaworthy even if it *was* seaworthy since he lacked adequate grounds for the belief. He was intellectually careless and was probably indulging in wishful thinking. In that case and in the guessing case, a true belief is not enough to be knowledge because it is not *good* enough to be knowledge.

This is the third relatively uncontroversial feature of knowledge: Knowledge is epistemically better than true belief. It is doubtful that philosophers would have given so much attention to the difference between knowledge and true belief in the history of philosophy if they did not make that assumption. I suggest that it is an assumption we should accept.

This brings us to the controversial component of knowledge. There are lots of ways a true belief can be good, better than true belief simpliciter. Which one is relevant to knowledge? The examples above suggest that the way knowing is better than true believing has something to do with the way the belief is acquired or the grounds upon which it is based. The belief must be acquired or held in an epistemically good way; guessing is definitely not an epistemically good way to get a belief. The belief must also be epistemically conscientious; believing your ship is seaworthy without any evidence is not epistemically conscientious. The three definitions of knowledge at the beginning of the chapter are designed in part to rule out these kinds of cases.

We looked at another approach to identifying the distinctive good of knowledge in Chapter One. Certainty and understanding are epistemic values each of which has dominated philosophical discourse for long periods of history, and they have both had important influences on the way knowledge has been understood. So knowledge might be true belief with certainty, or alternatively, it might be true belief with understanding.

---

[6] The lucky guess is a classic example of a true belief that is not knowledge, but would anybody believe on the basis of a guess? Guessing is a process that normally carries with it the awareness that it is guessing, so its unreliability should be transparent to the mind of the guesser. But even if nobody ever believes on the basis of a guess, the example can still be used to show that mere true belief cannot be sufficient for knowledge. Those readers who think it matters that people do not actually believe by guessing might want to think of other examples of hitting on the truth in a way that is random, and where believing the result is more psychologically realistic.

Adding these last two definitions to the three with which we began makes the task of defining knowledge even more confusing. There are lots of ways a true belief can be good and lots of epistemic states we value. Maybe there is no single state that is *really* knowledge, but there are lots of different states that different philosophers call knowledge, each of which is good in some way. That is a possibility, but it is too soon to give up on the task of defining knowledge in a way that both respects the tradition and is compatible with the intuitions ordinary people have. Still, we probably should be on notice that wherever we end up in our attempt to identify the components of knowledge, we may have to give up something in either intuition or the tradition.

Let us return to the two types of true belief that fail to be knowledge. One is the true belief that gets to the truth by luck. The other is the true belief that is unconscientious. Both are true beliefs that do not seem to be good enough to be knowledge, but they fail to be good enough in somewhat different ways. An epistemically unconscientious belief is one that arises from or expresses a disvaluing of truth on the part of the epistemic agent. Even if such a belief is true, it is lacking something epistemically good. Good epistemic luck is different. Luck is a good thing, or at least it is not a bad thing. If a believer gets to the truth by luck, there is nothing bad about the luck *per se*. Nonetheless, the believer does not seem to deserve the accolade "knowledge" because she lacks *merit* for her attainment of truth.

These two ways a true belief can lack something good can easily be connected. A believer may lack merit for getting the truth because she was epistemically unconscientious in getting the belief, and being epistemically conscientious is a way that she can get merit for getting the truth, but it is possible that there are other ways. We will return to these two types of cases again as we proceed with evaluating different proposals on what knowledge is.

II. THE VALUE PROBLEM

In this chapter we will work toward a definition of knowledge in stages. We have passed the first and easiest stage, and have concluded that knowing is believing a true proposition in a good way. That means that no definition of knowledge is adequate if it does not identify a feature of knowledge that makes it better than mere true belief. In other work I have called the problem of what makes knowledge better than true belief **the value problem**.[7] In this section we will begin with the second definition of knowledge proposed above, and I will argue that simple forms of reliabilism fail because they do not give a satisfactory answer to the value problem. Some other theories fail for the same reason. The argument of this section will allow us to draw some morals for the way we should construct a definition of knowledge.

Definition (ii) is the simplest version of reliabilism and it reveals the basic structure of reliabilist theories: Knowledge is true belief that is the output of a reliable belief-forming process. Given our general schema for defining knowledge, one difficulty arises immediately: Reliability *per se* has no value or disvalue. A reliable process is good only because of the good of the product of the process. A reliable espresso maker is good because espresso is good. A reliable water-dripping faucet is not good because dripping water is not good. The value or disvalue of a reliable source derives solely from the value or disvalue of that which it reliably produces. So the value of the product of a process is transferred to the process that produces it, but the value of the process is not transferred back again to the product. A reliable espresso maker is good because espresso is good, but the espresso made now does not get any better in virtue of the fact that it was produced by a reliable espresso machine. If the espresso tastes good, it makes no difference if it comes from an unreliable machine.

Similarly, a reliable truth-producing process is good because true belief is good. But if I acquire a true belief from such a process, that does not make my true belief better than it would be otherwise. Of course, since the process is good, I am better off for having it, and I may be better off for using it on a particular occasion, but that does not add epistemic status to any given true belief of mine that it produces.

One moral to draw from this example is that value can be transferred in one direction only, not back and forth. The value of the product is transferred to the value of a process reliably producing that

---

[7] I mention the value problem briefly in Zagzebski (1996), pp. 301–304, and first discuss it in some detail in Zagzebski (2000), reprinted in an expanded version in Axtell (2000). Another version of the value problem is proposed by Michael DePaul (1993) and (2001b). See also Kvanvig (2003). This section of the chapter is largely taken from Zagzebski (2000) and (2003b).

product, but the product in any given case does not get an extra boost of value from the value of the process. So the value of true belief makes a reliable truth-producing process good, but a particular true belief does not get any extra value from being the product of such a process. Hence, process reliabilism cannot explain what gives knowledge greater value than true belief. If knowledge is true belief + x, x cannot be the property of being the product of a reliable truth-producing process.

As we saw in Chapter Two, there are versions of reliabilism that identify knowledge with true belief resulting from reliable faculties or agents. As developed by Sosa and Greco, these theories are more complicated than simple reliabilism, but notice that if the good-making feature of a belief-forming faculty or agent is only its reliability, then faculty reliabilism and agent reliabilism have the same problem as process reliabilism; being the product of a reliable faculty or agent does not add value to the product.[8] This, then, is the first moral we will draw from the value problem: *Truth plus a reliable source of truth cannot explain the value of knowledge.*

The problem for reliabilism, then, is that whatever makes the product of a reliable faculty good cannot be reliability, but something else. A reasonable suggestion is that that something else underlies and explains the reliability of the faculty or process. So even if reliabilists are right that there is a close connection between reliably formed true beliefs and knowledge, the source of the value of knowledge must be something deeper than reliability, and the x feature of knowing cannot be identical with reliability.

Suppose we succeed in identifying such a value. Is that sufficient to solve the value problem? Not necessarily. Alvin Plantinga's proper function theory, a successor to reliabilism, is an attempt to identify something valuable that is deeper than reliability and that explains it. Typically, a reliable faculty is reliable because it is properly functioning, the way it was designed, whereas an unreliable faculty is unreliable because it is improperly functioning. Arguably, proper functioning is what is really valuable in our belief-forming

---

[8] Sosa and Greco usually have particular faculties and properties of agents in mind, properties they call virtues, for example, a good memory, keen eyesight, and well-developed powers of reasoning. Arguably, the goodness of these virtues is not limited to their reliability, and as long as that is recognized, the theory has a way out of the value problem. For this reason these theories are not forms of pure reliabilism. In recent work Sosa and Greco have proposed forms of the credit theory, discussed later in the chapter.

faculties, not reliability *per se*. This insight led Plantinga (1993, p. 59) to propose the following definition of knowledge (leaving out some details):

> (iv) Knowledge is true belief produced by properly functioning faculties in an appropriate environment according to a design plan aimed at truth.

Notice, however, that a properly functioning faculty, like a reliable faculty, gets its value from what it does or produces when it is functioning properly. A properly functioning cancer cell is not good even though it is functioning properly *for* a cancer cell. It may be a good cancer cell, but it is not good. Properly functioning nerve gas is not good even though it is functioning as nerve gas is supposed to function. Cancer cells and nerve gas are not good; in fact, proper functioning makes them even worse.

But Plantinga's definition of knowledge includes a crucial feature that might permit him to avoid this objection. What gives properly functioning faculties additional value, in Plantinga's theory, is that they are the product of intelligent design that has a certain aim. Plantinga can say that a properly functioning espresso machine is good, not only because espresso is good, but because it has fulfilled the purpose of its designer. Perhaps this gives the machine value in addition to the value of its product. So if my espresso machine is functioning properly, it is a good machine because it is doing what it is designed to do. It is not good simply because espresso is good. A malfunctioning faucet is bad because it is not doing what it is designed to do, and its badness is not merely derivative from the badness of dripping water; or so it can be argued.

But is the value of the espresso produced by a machine functioning as it was designed any better than it would be if it were produced by a machine that is not functioning as designed? I don't think it is. If the result is just as good, it makes no difference if the process was one designed to be used in that way. The fact that things and processes operate as designed may be a good thing, but it is a good extrinsic to the product. The product itself is neither better nor worse insofar as it is the product of design. This leads us to a second moral of the value problem: *Truth plus an independently valuable source is not sufficient to explain the value of knowledge.*

This is an interesting result because it forces us to think about the relevance of the relationship between a true belief and its source. Both reliabilists and Plantinga often speak of a source of belief and the belief it produces on the model of a machine and its product. If the machine that produces the product has certain properties, then the product allegedly has certain good properties. My analogy with an espresso machine and the espresso it produces follows that model, and I have argued that on that model, we cannot explain how it is that true belief gets good properties from the belief-forming machine that produces it. But we probably have that reaction in the espresso example because a cup of espresso is not an intrinsic component of the espresso maker. There are other cases in which we *do* think that valuable properties of a cause transfer to the effect, for instance, when the cause is an agent and the effect is an act. That is because an act is not an object independent of the agent who brings it about; it is part of the agent. There are important respects in which a state of knowing is like an act and, in fact, some philosophers have thought that knowing is an act of a certain kind.[9]

I will return to the analogy between acts and states of knowing, but at this point I think we can conclude that whether or not knowing is an act, if the value of knowing has something to do with its source, then knowing is a part of the agent, unlike a cup of espresso, which is not a part of the espresso maker. This leads to a third moral of the value problem: *Knowing is not related to the knower as product to machine, but is an intrinsic part of the knowing agent.*

Let us now turn to definition (i) at the beginning of this chapter: Knowledge is justified true belief. Whether this definition also succumbs to the value problem depends upon what is meant by "justified" and what makes a justified belief good. In many traditional justified-true-belief (JTB) theories, a belief is justified just in case it is based upon adequate evidence. But if basing belief on evidence is good only because doing so reliably leads to the truth, then the good of a justified belief is no different than the good of a belief arising from a reliable or truth-conducive process, in which case the definition does not explain what makes knowledge better than true belief.[10]

On the other hand, justification might be good in itself, not only because justification is a truth-conducive state. If so, the JTB definition of knowledge would escape the problem that plagues

[9] The idea that knowing is an act was more common in ancient and medieval philosophy than in contemporary philosophy. I argued that we should think of knowing as an act in Zagzebski (2003b).

[10] Laurence BonJour does that in BonJour (1985), pp. 7–8. See Chapter Two of Michael DePaul (1993) for an insightful discussion of BonJour and others in explaining the value of knowledge.

reliabilism. Furthermore, a theory of justification might include the idea that basing a belief on evidence includes seeing the connection between the evidence and the truth. So when a person bases a true belief on the evidence, it is good that she has the truth; it is good that she has evidence; it is an additional good that her true belief is based upon the evidence. The fact that she bases her belief on the evidence is good, not only because doing so leads to the truth in general, nor because it has led to the truth on this occasion, but because on this occasion she has seen the connection between the evidence and the true proposition she believes, and has thereby acquired a level of epistemic status she would not have had otherwise.

That explains why we think that there is something epistemically valuable about even a false belief properly based on evidence. In contrast, it is problematic to say that there is something epistemically valuable about a false belief produced by a reliable process. Would we say that the bad-tasting espresso produced by a reliable espresso maker is any better than bad-tasting espresso produced by an unreliable espresso maker? I doubt it, and for that reason I doubt that we would say that the false belief produced by a reliable truth-producing process is any better than the false belief produced by an unreliable belief process. This is another indication of the value problem inherent in reliabilism: If a reliable process does not give value to a false belief, it does not add value to a true belief either.

It seems, then, that the definition of knowledge as justified true belief cannot be faulted for not identifying a distinct epistemic good in addition to getting the truth, at least not if it is interpreted as I have suggested. Unfortunately, there is another problem with defining knowledge as belief that is true + justified, and this problem has an even broader reach of failed definitions than the value problem. This is the famous Gettier problem, the topic of the next section.

III. GETTIER

In 1963 Edmund Gettier published a two-page paper in *Analysis* that became one of the most famous philosophy papers in the last half century. Once he published the paper, he dropped the issue and showed no interest in the massive literature he generated. The paper was called "Is Justified True Belief Knowledge?" Gettier's paper contained two counterexamples to definition (i), which at that time was the most common definition of knowledge on offer. Definitions (ii) and (iii) and many others have been proposed since Gettier, and I will argue that most of them fall prey to Gettier's style of counterexample. These examples might sound artificial and strained to some students, but I think they will permit us to draw an important moral for the way definitions of knowledge should be constructed. Even though the examples do not sound like the sort of thing that can teach us anything significant about knowledge, if we delve into these cases with care, I think we find something surprising, or so I will argue in this section.

Gettier begins his paper by noting two points that he implies are needed to generate his counterexamples: (1) It is possible to be justified in believing a proposition that is false, and (2) if S is justified in believing p and p entails q and S believes q by deducing q from p, then S is justified in believing q.[11]

Here is one of Gettier's famous examples. Imagine that Smith has strong evidence that Jones owns a Ford. He has seen Jones driving a Ford on many occasions, and Jones has told him that he owns a Ford. (You may imagine that he has further evidence if you think it is needed for justification.) So Smith is justified in believing

(A) Jones owns a Ford.

Imagine also that Smith is totally ignorant of the whereabouts of his friend Brown, but from (A) Smith deduces:

(B) Either Jones owns a Ford or Brown is in Barcelona.

(Don't ask what would possess Smith to draw such an inference.)

Imagine now that in fact (A) is false. Jones lied to Smith and is presently driving a rented car, but by sheer coincidence, Brown is in Barcelona. (B) is true and given assumptions (1) and (2), Smith is justified in believing (B), but Smith does not know (B). Hence, definition (i) is mistaken. Justified true belief is not sufficient for knowledge.

Why do we think that Smith does not know (B)? Actually, I have encountered students who think that Smith does know (B),[12] but upon reflection most agree that there is something epistemically

---

[11] Gettier does not say that these two assumptions are necessary for generating counterexamples to the JTB definition of knowledge, but he says he is making these assumptions in order to give his examples.

[12] I suspect that those students have a different view about lucky true beliefs than is usual among philosophers. The place of luck in knowledge is attracting more attention in contemporary epistemology. See, for instance Pritchard (2005) and Riggs (2007).

defective about Smith's belief (B), something significant enough that his belief does not reach the status of a state of knowledge. What seems to go wrong is that in spite of the fact that Smith has conscientiously attempted to reach the truth and he does reach the truth, he does not get to the truth through his conscientious epistemic activity. It is bad luck that he is the unwitting victim of Jones's lies; it is only an accident that a procedure that usually leads to the truth leads him to the falsehood (A). Smith ends up with a true belief (B) anyway due to a second accidental feature of the situation, a feature that has nothing to do with Smith. I would describe the case as one in which an accident of bad luck is cancelled out by an accident of good luck. The truth is attained, but it is attained by luck.

Once we notice the double-luck structure of Gettier cases, we can see that the problem arises for a very wide range of definitions, including (ii) and (iii) above and many others. If knowledge is true belief + x, it does not matter whether x is identified with justification, reliability, proper function, conscientiousness, intellectual virtue, or something else. It does not matter whether x is an internalist element or an externalist element. It does not matter whether qualifications are added to definitions like (i). As we will see, the problem arises out of the *relation* between x and the truth in any definition according to which it is possible to have a false belief that is x.

For convenience, epistemologists sometimes call the x feature of knowledge warrant, so knowledge is true warranted belief. According to most accounts of warrant, a false warranted belief is possible; to say otherwise would be implausibly stringent. For example, philosophers who identify warrant with justification do not claim that if a belief is justified it must be true. A belief may be justified in the degree sufficient for knowledge when the belief is true even though it is possible for a belief to be equally justified but false. Presumably it does not happen very often that a belief is justified in the degree required for knowledge when it is false, but it can happen. Justification does not guarantee truth.

Similarly, philosophers who identify warrant with reliability or proper function typically do not claim that if a belief is true and warranted in the degree sufficient for knowledge, then any belief that is warranted in that degree is true. For example, when Plantinga defines a warranted belief as a belief produced by properly functioning faculties in the appropriate environment according to a design plan aimed at truth, he does not mean to require that faculties must be working perfectly in an environment perfectly matched to them.

Similarly, reliabilists do not require that a belief-forming process or faculty be perfectly reliable, only that the process or faculty is generally truth-conducive. Presumably, all these theories of warrant assume a close connection between warrant and truth, so a warranted false belief is not usual, but it is possible. A person with very good eyesight in good light in a normal environment may form a false belief based on visual perception because good eyesight is not perfect eyesight; properly functioning eyesight is not perfectly functioning eyesight. Warrant interpreted as reliability or proper function does not guarantee truth.

But with the common assumption that a warranted false belief is possible, the double-luck feature of Gettier's Smith example above allows us to produce a general recipe for generating counterexamples. First, find an example of a false warranted belief according to the account of warrant you are considering. The falsity of the belief will be due to some element of bad luck in the scenario since we assume that warranted beliefs are closely correlated with truth. Next, amend the case by adding another element of luck, only this time an element that makes the belief true after all. The second element must be independent of the element of warrant so that the degree of warrant is unchanged. The result is that one element of luck counteracts another. We then have an example in which a belief is true and is warranted in a sense strong enough for knowledge, but is not knowledge. The conclusion is that as long as the concept of knowledge as warranted true belief closely connects the elements of truth and warrant but permits some degree of independence between them, not every warranted true belief will be an instance of knowledge.

Is there any way to save definitions (i)–(iv) from Gettier-style counterexamples? In the Smith example, he infers (B) from justified false belief (A). This feature of Gettier's examples led some writers after Gettier to suggest that the solution to the Gettier problem is to stipulate that there be no false belief in the subject's evidence class.[13] However, this move is not sufficient to avoid Gettier problems because even though the recipe I have given for generating Gettier cases depends upon the possibility of a warranted false belief, it is not necessary for the counterexample that the subject actually have the false belief in question.

---

[13] See Sosa (1974) and Lehrer and Paxson (1969), both of which can be found in Pappas and Swain (1978). For a recent defense of this view, see William Lycan (2006), which can be found in Hetherington (2006).

Let us see how a subject can have a true warranted belief that is not knowledge without inferring the belief from a false belief. Suppose Dr. Jones, a reliable and highly competent physician, has excellent inductive evidence that her patient, White, is suffering from virus V1. White exhibits all of the symptoms of V1, and let us imagine that this particular set of symptoms is not associated with any other known virus. Suppose that all of the evidence upon which Jones bases her diagnosis is true; she believes it and is warranted in believing it, and there is no evidence accessible to her that would count significantly against her conclusion that White is suffering from virus V1. The conclusion that White is suffering from V1 really is extremely probable on the evidence. Dr. Jones believes he is suffering from V1 and is warranted in her belief.

But suppose now that the symptoms White exhibits are actually caused by a very rare and unknown virus V2, which has exactly the same symptoms as virus V1. However, White has just contracted virus V1 also, but so recently that he does not yet have any symptoms caused by V1. In the particular case, there is no connection between the evidence upon which Jones bases her diagnosis that White has V1 and the fact that he has V1. Her belief that White has virus V1 is true and warranted, but it is not knowledge. Furthermore, Dr. Jones's belief is not based upon a false belief. All the evidence upon which she bases her belief is true.

Now you might think that Dr. Jones has the false belief that White's symptoms are caused by virus V1, but she need not have that belief. She may be a very careful inductive reasoner. She draws no inferences about causes. She merely knows the high correlation between White's symptoms and virus V1, and upon that basis, she concludes that White has virus V1. We are assuming that it really *is* objectively probable that White has virus V1 since virus V2 is extremely rare. Perhaps only one in ten thousand cases of symptoms like White's are due to virus V2. Dr. Jones does not know of the existence of virus V2, but she knows that there is much that she does not know about viruses and their symptoms, so she is not certain that White has virus V1, and that is the right epistemic attitude. However, since certainty is not required for warrant, at least not in the range of accounts of knowledge we are considering, her lack of certainty does not diminish her warrant for believing White has virus V1. Yet Jones does not know White has V1 because the truth of her belief is not connected with her evidence in the right way.

This example follows the recipe I gave above for producing Gettier cases because the case is constructed in two stages: (1) Find a scenario with a warranted false belief, in this case, a scenario like the one above except that White has not contracted virus V1, and (2) add a wrinkle to the case that makes the belief come out true after all, in this case, by adding the feature that White has just recently contracted virus V1. The recipe requires the possibility of a warranted false belief in a closely related scenario, but in the actual scenario, there is no false belief upon which Dr. Jones bases her Gettierized belief.

The Dr. Jones case shows that Gettier did not need his second assumption for generating counterexamples. Recall that Gettier begins his paper by noting two points that he implies are needed for his cases to work: (1) It is possible to be justified in believing a proposition that is false, and (2) if S is justified in believing p and p entails q and S believes q by deducing q from p, then S is justified in believing q. He goes on to give two cases in which the subject is justified in believing a false proposition p, and then validly deduces a justified true proposition q that intuitively is not knowledge. But in the Dr. Jones case, her warrant (and justification) for believing that White has virus V1 is not based on drawing an inference from a false belief. The only supposition needed to get a case like Dr. Jones is Gettier's first assumption (1).

A wide range of definitions of knowledge fall prey to counterexamples like the case of Dr. Jones and Gettier cases. Gettier directed his examples at definition (i), but I have argued that the recipe I propose can be used to produce counterexamples to definition (ii) and related definitions. What about definition (iii) and other contextualist accounts of knowledge? Definitions that involve relevant alternatives are qualifications or amendments to some *other* definition of knowledge, restricting or expanding the range of evidence needed to reach the level of knowledge to what is relevant in the context or what the subject cares about. It seems to me that definitions of this kind face the same counterexamples as the definitions they amend as long as it is possible for a false belief to meet the criteria for x in the schema: Knowledge = true belief + x. The recipe I propose for generating Gettier counterexamples is general enough that it applies to any definition of knowledge that fits the above schema and which permits a false x belief.

I think this shows that there is something wrong with all of the definitions of knowledge we have considered so far. What can we do? The laziest response would be to keep our preferred definition of knowledge, whatever it may be, and tack on the amendment "and is not a Gettier case." For example, if you like definition (i), you could amend your definition as follows:

(i′) Knowledge is justified true belief that is not a Gettier case.

If you like (ii) instead, you could amend it in a parallel fashion:

(ii′) Knowledge is true belief that arises from a reliable belief-forming process and is not a Gettier case.

Clearly, you could make the same move for any definition you like. But how satisfying would such a definition be? If you think that the believer does not have knowledge in a Gettier situation, there must be some feature of the situation that gives you that intuition, and it is important to identify that feature, since it tells us something about the nature of knowledge. And even if what it tells us is not particularly important, we won't know that until we have identified the source of the worry in Gettier situations.

A better response to Gettier cases is to look more carefully at the assumptions that generate the problem. We have been operating with the assumption that we can divide the components of knowledge in a very general way as true belief + x. We also assumed that a false x belief is possible. If we follow the convention of calling x "warrant," we are assuming that a false warranted belief is possible. That is, it is possible that there is a belief that is warranted in the degree that is sufficient to convert a true belief into knowledge, but is false. That means there is a degree of independence between the truth of the belief and warrant. Presumably, warrant is closely connected to truth, but it does not guarantee it.

We could, of course, deny that there is any significant connection between warrant and truth, so whenever a believer has a warranted belief that is true, it is luck that the belief is true. With such an approach, knowledge would be mostly luck anyway, so Gettier cases would not generate any worries. We would simply accept them as cases of knowledge. In my experience, not many people find this an appealing way to go.

We are now left with only one solution: *Close the gap between warrant and truth.* The conclusion is that warrant entails truth.

There are, however, two very different ways to close the gap, and it is important that they not be confused. One way would be to accept the model of knowledge as true belief + warrant, where warrant is some feature that a belief has that guarantees its truth. This approach has traditionally been called **infallibilism**. The most important proponent of infallibilism in the history of philosophy is Descartes, who argued that necessarily, if I clearly and distinctly perceive p, then p is true. As every student of philosophy knows, his fundamental example of a clear and distinct perception is "I think, therefore, I am."

The possibility of having beliefs with a feature that guarantees their truth is fascinating, but unfortunately, we have no reason to think that very many of our beliefs have this feature, so if having such a feature is a necessary condition for knowledge, we have very little knowledge. I think, then, that the infallibilist way of closing the gap between warrant and truth is unlikely to give us a satisfactory account of knowledge, but it is worth noticing that Cartesian infallibilism does not have Gettier problems.

Fortunately, there is another way to close the gap. We have been operating with the assumption that knowledge is composed of two distinct components, one of which is truth, and the other of which is the mysterious x, which we have dubbed "warrant" for convenience. But if truth is a component of warrant itself, warrant entails truth without implying an excessively stringent and implausible infallibilism. Here are some examples of this way of closing the gap between warrant and truth:

(i″) Knowledge is belief that gets to the truth because it is justified.

(ii″) Knowledge is belief that gets to the truth because it arises from a reliable belief-forming process.

(iii″) Knowledge is belief that gets to the truth because it is supported by evidence that eliminates all possibilities except for the ones we are properly ignoring.

(iv″) Knowledge is belief that gets to the truth because it arises from properly functioning faculties in an appropriate environment according to a design plan aimed at truth.

In each of the above definitions, warrant is the property of getting to the truth because of a putative good-making feature of the belief or the belief process. Truth is entailed by warrant because truth is a component of warrant, not because there is some property of a belief that is independent of truth but guarantees it.[14]

---

[14] The Howard-Snyders (2003) misunderstand my position as a form of infallibilism, and their interpretation is repeated by Lycan (2006).

Gettier cases therefore show us something surprising. Our initial formula for defining knowledge as true belief + x is a mistake, or at least misleading. We should not think of knowledge as composed of true belief plus some other independent component. Putting together the ingredients of knowledge is more like mixing a cake than mixing a salad. A cake typically includes butter, sugar, eggs, and flour, but the cake will not turn out well unless the ingredients are mixed in a certain way. The butter and sugar must be creamed to a certain consistency before the flour is added. A Gettier case is like a cake that has the right ingredients, but they are not mixed together in the right way, and the result is not a good cake. The structure of knowledge may not be very complicated, but it is more complicated than simply the collection of a couple of ingredients like true belief and warrant. Knowledge is not truth plus warrant, and for the same reason warrant is not knowledge minus truth. My own view is that there is not much use for the concept of warrant, but I will continue to use it occasionally in discussing other theories.

The schema for defining knowledge given in definitions (i'')–(iv'') is not the only way to close the gap between warrant and truth in order to avoid Gettier counterexamples. Another way is the strong **defeasibility theory**.[15] Roughly, this theory maintains that S knows p if and only if S believes p, p is true and justified, and there is no true proposition q which if added to S's evidence for p would make p unjustified. If p is false, there are many other propositions that are logically or evidentially connected to p that are false also. Should S come to believe any of these propositions, S's belief p would be unjustified. Therefore, no false proposition can satisfy the defeasibility condition and the truth condition in the definition is redundant. The defeasibility theory therefore defines knowledge roughly as follows:

> (v) S knows p if and only if S justifiably believes p and there is no true proposition q such that if S should come to believe q, S's belief p would be unjustified.

Notice that my recipe for generating Gettier counterexamples does not apply to this definition, since (v) closes the gap between warrant and truth. I will not discuss (v) further since I want to take another approach, but I want to point out an interesting feature of it. Notice that it is strongly externalist. Whether S knows p is determined from the standpoint of an omniscient observer.

---

[15] Examples can be found in Lehrer (1965), Klein (1976), and Swain (1978).

Let us now combine the moral of the Gettier problem with the morals of the value problem.

(1) Knowledge should be defined in such a way that the truth component cannot be separated from its other component. Definitions (i″)–(iv″) and (v) are examples of ways to do that.

(2) The feature of knowledge other than truth should be something epistemically good, something that makes the resulting state better than true belief. I do not think definition (ii″) satisfies this restriction.

The last two sections have shown us some restrictions on an acceptable definition of knowledge, and we have applied these restrictions to several definitions that have appeared in the literature over the last few decades. Three definitions that survive have a common form. Definitions (i″), (iii″), and (iv″) are specifications of the following definition schema:

DS: Knowledge is belief in which the believer gets to the truth because of her good epistemic behavior.

The relation *A because of B* is the key element in the approach to avoiding Gettier problems I have endorsed. This relation is an important one for many philosophical theses, not just the definition of knowledge, but it resists analysis. To say A occurs because B occurs suggests a causal relation between B and A, but the causal relation resists analysis also, and in any case, the because-of relation is probably broader than the causal relation. Some philosophers have attempted an account of the causal relation in terms of counterfactual conditionals, and it would be interesting to compare attempts at defining knowledge in terms of counterfactual conditionals with DS.[16]

If the believer gets to the truth because she is doing what is epistemically right or good, we can say that she deserves *credit* for getting the truth. Conversely, if she deserves credit, there has to be something epistemically good about her in virtue of which she gets the credit. The notion of credit is closely connected to achieving an end through something good in the agent. The notion of credit for

---

[16] Some of the theories that use counterfactual conditionals propose conditions of "sensitivity" or "safety." For examples of sensitivity, see Dretske (1971) and Nozick (1981), and for examples of safety, see Sosa (2000) and Pritchard (2005).

the truth is closely connected to achieving the truth through something epistemically good in the agent. This leads us to the last set of definitions of knowledge I want to consider in this chapter.[17]

IV. CREDIT THEORIES OF KNOWLEDGE

Here is a general definition of knowledge that avoids Gettier problems and arguably avoids the value problem:

> (vi) Knowledge is true belief in which the believer is credited with getting the truth.

Wayne Riggs (1998), John Greco (2003), and Ernest Sosa (2003) have proposed definitions that are variations of (vi).

It is not clear whether (vi) has the value problem because the notion of credit is vague. I argued above that the espresso in the cup is not made better by the fact that it is produced by a reliable espresso maker or a properly functioning espresso maker, and for the same reason, it does not get any better if the machine gets credit for producing the espresso. That is to say, the coffee in the cup does not taste any better. That suggests that if I am related to my beliefs as the espresso maker is related to the cup of espresso, (vi) does not escape the value problem. However, I think that (vi) avoids the problem provided that it is combined with a view of knowledge that rejects the machine-product model discussed earlier.[18]

The notion of credit needs to be filled out with an account of the relevant way in which a believer gets credit for the truth of her beliefs. I suggest that credit for true belief can be understood on the model of credit for good acts. Let me sketch a way that I think that can be done. The account I am about to give segues into the account of conscientious belief given in the last chapter. I don't claim that this account is the only way the credit theory can go, but I think it is promising.

An act gets moral value from its motives in addition to any value it has from its consequences and from the fact that the act is

---

[17] My discussion of Gettier cases in this section is partly taken from Zagzebski (1994) and (1996).

[18] As far as I can tell, Greco and Riggs reject the machine-product model, but Sosa often uses it, for example, in Sosa (2003), in which he proposes his way out of the value problem.

intentionally an act of a certain kind. I do not want to insist that acts necessarily get moral value from their consequences, and I will not discuss the concept of an intentional act, but I want to argue that motives add to the value of acts. What I mean by a motive is an emotional state that can cause the agent to act in a way that aims at bringing about an end characteristic of the motive in question. A motive in my sense is not the only cause of an act, but it is causally operative and I maintain that it gives the agent credit for the act it motivates. Let me illustrate this claim with an example.

Roughly, the motive of benevolence is caring about the well-being of others. A person can bring about the well-being of another unintentionally, but we think that the moral value of the act is greater if it is motivated by benevolence. For instance, suppose that when Molly goes to visit her cousin, her elderly aunt overhears her telling an amusing story to her cousin and that cheers her up. Molly does not intend any benefit to her aunt and is unaware of the connection between telling her story and its good consequence. Molly's behavior may have value deriving from its consequence, but we would not say that she gets credit for her aunt's improved well-being. Since the idea of credit is vague, there is possibly a sense in which she does get credit. But there is also an important sense in which it is accidental that she improves her aunt's well-being, so any merit she gets for the consequence of her act is minimal at best.

Our reaction is quite different if Molly acts intentionally to improve her aunt's well-being, motivated by caring about her aunt's welfare. Her motive of benevolence gives her moral credit for the good she produces. But we can distinguish a case in which Molly cares about her aunt's welfare as such from one in which she cares about her aunt's welfare because she thinks that the well-being of others is instrumentally connected to her own well-being. I think that in both cases Molly acts from a motive of benevolence and gets moral credit for making her aunt cheerful, but the morally superior act is the one in which she cares about the well-being of her aunt as such. She gets more moral credit in the latter case.[19]

---

[19] My claims that the motive of benevolence does not require valuing the welfare of others for its own sake and that an agent gets moral credit for acting out of benevolence in this sense are related to a point Aristotle makes at the end of the *Eudemian Ethics*. There Aristotle compares people who are plain good (*agathos*) and people who are both good and noble (*kalos kakgathos*). Only the latter value virtue for its own sake. I discuss this distinction in Zagzebski (1996), p. 317.

We can use these three cases to look at corresponding degrees of credit for achieving true belief. In the first case we can suppose that Molly gets a true belief accidentally. She has a fleeting glimpse of a man in a grey jacket in the library and identifies him as Jim, and let's imagine that the man is, in fact, Jim, although she could easily have mistaken any of a dozen men in the library for Jim. The fact that Molly has a true belief is a good thing, assuming that true belief is a good thing, but Molly does not get credit for achieving the truth any more than she gets credit for improving her aunt's well-being when she does so accidentally.

Suppose, however, that Molly is writing about the library for her town newspaper and is attentive, careful, and thorough in her research. She values getting the truth, and she conducts her research in a way aimed at that result, and let's suppose that in doing so she succeeds in finding out that there is a photograph of Jim's grand-mother on the library wall. This is parallel to the situation in which she values her aunt's welfare, acts in a way aimed at that result, and succeeds in doing so because of these features of the act.

But just as there is a difference between caring about the well-being of others for its own sake and caring about the well-being of others as a means to some other good, there is also a difference between caring about the truth for its own sake and caring about the truth as a means to some other good, for example, enhancing her reputation. Molly might care about getting a true story for the newspaper because she cares about the truth in itself, or because she wants to have a good reputation in the town. Is Molly conscientious in both cases?

In Chapter One I defined conscientiousness as caring about the truth, but I did not say that conscientiousness requires caring about the truth for its own sake. My argument that caring about anything commits us to caring about truth would be very implausible if it were interpreted as an argument that caring about something commits us to caring about truth for its own sake. The sense in which conscien-tiousness is demanded by caring about the things we care about cannot be so demanding. If so, Molly is conscientious and gets credit for reaching the truth in both of the above cases. Presumably, she gets more credit when she cares about getting a true story about the library for its own sake than when she thinks that the truth will enhance her reputation, but in both cases she gets credit for reaching the truth.

I think this shows that even though the notion of credit is vague, there is a close connection between (a) being conscientious in the behavior that gets us the truth, and (b) getting credit for the truth. If I am right about that, definition (vi) closely corresponds to:

(vii) Knowledge is belief in which the believer gets to the truth because she acts in an epistemically conscientious way.

According to both definitions, Molly does not have knowledge when she believes the man in the grey jacket is Jim, but she has knowledge when she believes that the photograph on the library wall depicts Jim's grandmother. I think that is the intuitively correct result. Of course, the examples above do not prove that definitions (vi) and (vii) coincide in all cases, but I think they indicate an intuitive connection between them. I will leave it to readers to consider examples of cases in which they may diverge.

Both definitions seem to me to be promising, but (vii) has the advantage of greater richness. It can be combined with an account of epistemic conscientiousness and the virtues that conscientious believers acquire to yield a richly substantive account of the nature of knowledge. In other work I have argued that knowledge is belief in which the truth is reached through intellectually virtuous motives and the cognitive acts they motivate (Zagzebski, 1996, Part III). If virtuous belief is connected with conscientious belief in the way I described in Chapter Four, then definition (vii) roughly coincides with the definition I have previously defended.[20]

It seems to me that (vi) and (vii) avoid the various hurdles we have encountered in producing a definition of the state of knowledge as long as (vi) is supplemented with an account of the relation between believer and belief to escape the value problem. Both also escape the Gettier problem, and both also explain why we think that true belief by luck and unconscientiously true belief are not instances of knowledge.

But we might wonder if they go too far. That is, even if (vi) or (vii) gives sufficient conditions for knowledge, does either one of them give necessary conditions? Aren't they too demanding? What about "easy knowledge," knowledge by simple perception or memory, or knowledge based on ordinary testimony? In such cases, does

[20] In Zagzebski (1996) I call an act of believing that gets to the truth because of the agent's intellectually virtuous motives and aims "an act of intellectual virtue." So knowing is an act of intellectual virtue. Roberts and Wood (2007, pp. 11–16) seem confused by this term and misunderstand my account of knowledge. Their attempt at a Gettier-style counterexample to my definition of knowledge (pp. 12–13) exhibits the confusion.

the believer get credit for reaching the truth? Perhaps definition (vi) is too demanding; in the case of memory and perception, it does not look like anybody gets credit, and in the case of testimony, it looks like the testifier is the one who gets the credit, if anybody does. Definition (vii) may seem too demanding also. Is conscientiousness necessary in cases of simple perceptual or memory knowledge or belief by testimony?[21]

I think our discussion of conscientiousness in Chapter Four shows that believing in a conscientious way does not always require intellectual discipline. We are conscientious when we have virtuous self-trust. We are permitted, even required, by the demands of conscientiousness to have basic trust in our epistemic faculties, including perceptual faculties, memory, and reasoning faculties, and I argued that we are also required to place basic trust in many other persons. What distinguishes the intellectually virtuous from the nonvirtuous believer is not the absence of trust in self and others, but the fact that trust is enhanced by virtues that limit and extend trust in the many ways I described in that chapter. An agent can act conscientiously on a particular occasion when she does not need to listen to contrary opinions because there aren't any. She does not need to be especially attentive because the circumstances are propitious for the perception upon which she bases her belief. She does not need to doubt her memory because there are no signs that indicate a reason not to trust it. She does not need to check the credentials of her informant because there is no reason to think that the person is unreliable.

According to (vii), what distinguishes easy knowledge from easy true belief that is not knowledge is that in a state of knowledge the believer gets to the truth *because* of her conscientious behavior and motives. Even though that does not require that she engage in the special cognitive discipline of the virtues when it is not called for, it does mean that she would do so in the relevant counterfactual circumstances. Definition (vii) does not rule out easy knowledge by sense perception. A person who believes that she sees an easily identifiable object typically knows that she sees the object, provided that there are no indications in her environment that she should not trust her visual sense or understanding of the concept under which

---

[21] Ernest Sosa addresses this problem by distinguishing animal knowledge from reflective knowledge. See Sosa (1994b) and (2007).

the object falls. Definition (vii) does not rule out easy knowledge by testimony either. A person who believes on the basis of testimony that p by a testifier who knows p, and whose reliability she has no reason to doubt, knows p provided that she would not also believe p if she had reason to doubt the reliability of the testifier. That means that easy knowledge is not so easy that it collapses into easy true belief, but it seems to me that that is what we would want in an account of knowledge.

I think that parallel points apply to definition (vi), but I will leave it to interested readers to apply (vi) to individual cases.

In this chapter I have started to build a case for a close connection among the following: (a) getting credit for reaching the truth; (b) reaching the truth because of intellectually virtuous activity, including virtuous self-trust; and (c) reaching the truth because of epistemically conscientious behavior. I have not argued that (a)–(c) exactly coincide, and further work is needed to identify cases in which they diverge, but I think that this class of theories of knowledge is very promising.

In Chapter Four I presented a theory of epistemic normativity, a theory of the way we ought to govern our epistemic lives. In this chapter I have argued that once we see the way to govern our epistemic lives, we also see what knowledge is. Knowledge is a state of belief in which we get to the truth by governing our epistemic lives well.

FURTHER READING

Many epistemology texts focus on the analysis of knowledge, although there is a recent trend toward explicating other epistemic values as well. For a classic approach to the theory of knowledge, see Roderick Chisholm, *Theory of Knowledge* (Englewood Cliffs, NJ: Prentice Hall, 1977, 1989); the second and third editions differ in content somewhat and are both widely known. Michael Welbourne, *Knowledge* (Montreal: McGill-Queen's University Press, 2001) reviews several historical attempts (from Plato to modern philosophers) to analyze knowledge, and concludes with a unique analysis that incorporates the importance of testimony. More advanced students may want to read Edward Craig's *Knowledge and the State of Nature* (Oxford: Oxford University Press, 1990). Students should also

CHAPTER 5

read the very short, and highly influential, paper by Edmund Gettier, "Is Justified True Belief Knowledge?" *Analysis* 23 (121–23), which can be found in many anthologies. Advanced students interested in the value problem may want to take a look at Jonathan Kvanvig, *The Value of Knowledge and the Pursuit of Understanding* (Cambridge: Cambridge University Press, 2003). Duncan Pritchard's *Epistemic Luck* (Oxford: Oxford University Press, 2005) develops the importance of luck in epistemic contexts.

6

Epistemic Good and the Good Life

I. THE DESIRABILITY OF TRUTH

It is hard to imagine living a life without caring about many things. Even if it were possible, living without caring would not be a life we would care to live. Throughout this book I have emphasized that if we care about anything, we must care about truth in the domains we care about, as well as in domains about which caring is not optional, such as morality. In this chapter I want to go back to that claim and look more carefully at the relationship between caring about something and caring about truths related to it. What sort of connection is there between the value of truth and other things we value? More generally, what is the connection between truth and a good life? Under the assumption that knowledge is better than true belief, what does knowledge contribute to a good life? What about other epistemic values, such as understanding?

In Chapter One I argued that we require ourselves to care about truth, given that we care about other things. I did not argue that truth is valuable for its own sake, but I did not deny that either. In this section I want to look at these questions about the value of truth: (1) How does truth have value contingent upon other things we value? (2) Is truth also valuable for its own sake? (3) Is every true belief valuable all things considered? (4) What does the answer to these questions tell us about the value of knowledge?

It can be illuminating to divide the senses in which something can be good into the **desirable** and the **admirable**. The things that are desirable are the things that are good *for* us. They make us thrive as human beings. Examples include long life, health and freedom from suffering, comfort and the variety of human enjoyments, friendship and loving relationships, and using our talents in satisfying work. To say that these things are desirable is not to say that their desirability cannot be outweighed by other goods. Most desirable things are only prima facie desirable; they are not desirable at all costs. For one thing, given some set of contingent circumstances, one of these goods can conflict with another. The pleasures of a good life can harm our health; spending time with our friends can detract from creative activity; living an intellectually rich and creative life can be stressful. Living a healthy life can take time away from any of the other components of flourishing, including friends and creative activity, at least for those persons whose health requires considerable attention. Furthermore, some of these goods can conflict with morality. So to say that these goods are desirable is not to say that they are desirable in all circumstances, taking everything into consideration.

If true belief is desirable, it is desirable in the same way these other desirable aspects of a good life are desirable; it is prima facie desirable. The desirability of a given true belief can be defeated or outweighed by other features of a desirable life.[1] We cannot spend all our time pursuing truth, so we need to forego gaining some truths for the sake of other goods. We also know that some truths can hurt us. I don't know of any rule that tells us when suffering outweighs truth, but by saying that true belief is only prima facie desirable, I mean to

---

[1] I think there is a difference between a good that outweighs another good and a good that defeats another. When the goodness of A outweighs the goodness of B, the good of B is not taken away by the good of A. In contrast, when the goodness of A defeats the goodness of B, B's good is taken away by A; it is nullified. The easiest examples of the difference involve prima facie duties, for instance, the duty to keep promises. Suppose I tell a friend that I will meet her for lunch, but as I am leaving, I discover that my neighbor needs someone to take him to the hospital emergency room. The good of helping my neighbor outweighs the good of keeping my word to my friend to meet her for lunch, but the former does not nullify the latter. Even though I should take care of my neighbor first, I still owe my friend something in virtue of my promise—at a minimum, a telephone call as soon as I am able. But (to take an example from Plato's *Republic*) suppose that I borrow a knife and then discover that the lender wants it back in order to kill another person. The good of giving back his property is nullified by the bad of aiding him in committing a crime. The former good is defeated by the good of refusing any such assistance. The difference between outweighing and defeating might be interesting for some readers, but I will not pursue it in this chapter and will ignore it for the most part.

leave open the possibility that in particular cases, losing a truth can be better than getting it. It might even be better to have a false belief than a true one. Presumably, there are not many situations in which a false belief is better than a true one, given the strong connection between truth and the many things we care about, but I would not rule out the possibility that there are such cases.

The second way something can be good is in the sense of the admirable. I think of the admirable as the fitting object of the emotion of admiration. Moral and intellectual virtues are admirable, as well as aesthetic qualities and excellence in any area of human practice, including sports, science, and philosophy. If true belief is good, it is good in the sense of the desirable, not the admirable. If I am right that knowledge is something like credit for true belief, it is an achievement. It is good in the sense of the admirable. So knowledge is a state in which the believer gets to something desirable by being admirable.[2]

An important issue in moral philosophy is the relationship between a good life in these two senses. How is an admirable life, a life of virtue, related to a desirable life, a life of possession of the things that are good for us? In another place (Zagzebski, 2006b) I have argued that the admirable life is desirable. It is desirable to be admirable. I think it can be argued that knowledge is desirable, not only because it has a desirable component—true belief, but because it is desirable to get to the truth through intellectually admirable motives and behavior. But even if I am wrong in the latter claim, it is clear that if true belief is desirable, so is knowledge. And like the other desirable goods, there is no reason to think that knowledge is good absolutely; both knowledge and true belief are only prima facie desirable. The desirability of knowledge in a particular case can be defeated or outweighed by other desirable goods such as freedom from suffering and a satisfying life.

The analogous issue in ethics is this: Can the desirability of an act that is virtuous, and hence admirable, be defeated by other features of a desirable life? The ethical question is much harder than the epistemological analogue. I think it can be argued that the desirability of

---

[2] Credit seems to be a weaker evaluative notion than the admirable, but credit is in the same family as the admirable, not the desirable. When we give someone credit, we commend them. For those readers who think it is important that credit is weaker than the admirable, I suggest substituting "commendable" for "admirable" in my discussion of the two senses in which we call something good.

acting virtuously is never defeated by other desirable goods, but it would be implausible to argue that the desirability of knowledge is never defeated by the other desirable features of a good life. Even though knowledge always has an admirable, or at least, commendable feature, not every instance of knowledge is desirable all things considered. There might even be some objects of knowledge that are not worth knowing by anybody.

To see whether there is undesirable knowledge, let us go back to the relation between the desirability of truth and what we care about. Caring about something requires a cognitive relationship between us and the object of our caring. It is difficult to maintain a given level of caring without an input of information about the object of care. If I love the art of Duccio, I will find it hard to continue loving it if I stop looking at his paintings and learn nothing more about his art. In any case, caring about Duccio leads me to want to obtain information about his art. Presumably, I have no reason to do this obsessively because I care about a great many things more than Duccio's art, but other things being equal, the more I care, the greater the demand on me to acquire information about it. Is it good *for* me to get information about Duccio? I think it is, as long as it is good for me to care about Duccio, and I don't know why it couldn't be, given that we cannot live a good life without caring about many optional things, and I assume that caring about the art of Duccio is one of the options.

Furthermore, my caring about something puts a demand on me to get information about a lot of things that are instrumentally valuable to serving my interests in what I care about. Getting information about Duccio can serve a number of interests, some of which are nonepistemic. Maybe I want to pass an exam in an art history class or attract someone who loves art (like Woody Allen learning about Tintoretto in order to impress Julia Roberts in *Everyone Says I Love You*). Instrumental value is also a form of conditional value because the value of the means is conditional upon the value of the end we care about. As long as it can be good for someone to care about passing an exam or impressing an art expert, it is also good for him or her to care about truths that are instrumentally connected with those ends. So there are many truths that are good for us conditional upon the fact that (a) we care about certain things and (b) it is good for us to care about those things.

But surely not all true beliefs are good for us in this conditional sense. Many truths are trivial because they are about a domain we do not care about, and they are not instrumentally connected to anything we care about. Ernest Sosa gives the example of counting the grains of sand on the beach to illustrate his point that not every truth is worth having. Sosa (2001) observes that counting the grains of sand serves none of our interests. Actually, somebody *might* be interested in the number of grains of sand, and if she could get the answer with little effort, we probably would have no objection. But suppose that someone cares so much about the number of grains of sand that she is willing to spend an exorbitant amount of time in the effort to find the answer. Would we say that it is good for her to get the answer? Possibly we would, but it is more likely that we would wonder what is wrong with a person who would care so much about the trivial.

Some truths may be trivial for any being of our kind, just because we have the nature that we have. Someone who cares about the number of grains of sand on the beach may just have perverse interests for a human being. Her interests do not make believing the truth about the number of grains of sand desirable. In fact, we might think that there are two things undesirable about such a person: the triviality of her belief, and the perversity of her interest.

But for virtually any trivial truth we think of, there is some set of circumstances in which believing it and going through a long process of attempting to discover it is not trivial for somebody, and might not even be trivial for us taken collectively. I recently discovered that the ancient Greek mathematician, Archimedes (3rd cent. B.C.), wrote a treatise called *The Sand-Reckoner*, in which he devised a method for determining the upper bound for the number of grains of sand the universe theoretically could contain. (Using modern scientific notation, his answer is 8×10^{63}.) In order to make this calculation, Archimedes had to invent a method to use very large numbers since at the time, there was no method to express numbers larger than 10,000.[3] This is an interesting example because even if you think his question and its answer were trivial, the method he had to invent to get the answer clearly was not.

But in spite of surprising cases in which the apparently trivial turns out not to be trivial, it seems likely that there are many truths that really are trivial, no matter how you look at it. Many are trivial to a particular person, and some are probably trivial to everybody. Think

---

[3] Reviel Netz, a historian of mathematics, has argued that Archimedes could envisage actual infinity and was more sophisticated in his notions of infinity than the philosophers of the time. See the story "Eureka!" by Theresa Johnston in the *Stanford Magazine*, Sept./ Oct. 2007.

of all the mindless chatter to which you are subjected on a daily basis on television or at work. Even if the beliefs you pick up by these methods are true, they might not have prima facie desirability. If their desirability is conditional upon something you care about, they do not meet the condition.

There is still the possibility that every true belief is prima facie desirable simply because it is true.[4] Maybe there is something desirable about truth itself, regardless of what we care about. To have a true belief is to have your mind aligned with some bit of reality in the right way. Possibly this is always good for us, given the kind of beings that we are. If so, every true belief is prima facie good for us. It would follow that some true beliefs are good for us because of the relationship between the belief and things we care about; these are conditional goods. But in addition, maybe all true beliefs are good for us simply because the beliefs are true; their goodness is not conditional upon anything else.

I am willing to grant that every true belief is prima facie desirable just because it is true. Nonetheless, it is very unlikely that every true belief is desirable all things considered. As we have already noted, the fact that a belief is good for us can be defeated by other things that are good for us. Even if there is some value in every true belief that is not conditional upon something we care about, it does not follow that the value it has is very great. And as long as its value is only prima facie, it can be outweighed or defeated by other things.

The inescapable conclusion is that not every true belief is desirable, all things considered. Perhaps there are some beliefs that are always desirable for everybody, all things considered, but there are probably not many beliefs in this category. Some true beliefs are not good for us, and some true beliefs may even be bad for us. There are undesirable true beliefs. Since true beliefs are not in the category of things that are admirable, it follows that some true beliefs are not good in either sense, all things considered.

Notice what follows for the value of knowing. In Chapter Five I argued that some form of the credit theory of knowledge is the best on offer. According to the simplest form of that theory, knowing is believing in which the agent gets credit for getting the truth. Alternatively, knowing is believing in which the agent gets to the truth

---

[4] Kvanvig (2003, p. 41) and Lynch (2004, p. 55) suppose that it is. Lynch (forthcoming) also calls it "*pro-tanto* value."

through conscientious epistemic behavior. But if a given true belief is not desirable, what would be the point of giving the agent credit for it? And if some true beliefs are undesirable, it might even make more sense to say she is blamed for getting the truth than that she is praised for it. If every true belief is desirable insofar as it is true, it is desirable that the agent is credited with obtaining the truth, but the truth credited to her may not be much of a prize, and it is a prize that can be outweighed by other undesirable features of having the belief.

The same point applies to the proposal that knowing is achieving the truth through conscientious epistemic motives and acts. If some instance of truth, on balance, is not desirable, it is not clear why we should think it is desirable to achieve it by caring about the truth. If the value of a given true belief is low, then even if the value of believing it out of a love of truth is higher, how much higher can it get?

I would like to note an interpretation of the conscientiousness account of knowledge that would make it very implausible. We would not think that believing the truth is epistemically enhanced by caring about the truth of a *particular* belief when the truth of the particular belief is not desirable. Consider a case of "easy knowledge," discussed in Chapter Five. Suppose I notice a speck of dust on the floor of the library. I believe truly that there is a speck of dust, and under ordinary circumstances in which virtuous self-trust would not require me to do a special investigation to confirm my belief, I know that there is dust. My epistemic level is enhanced by self-trust governed by a general motive of love of truth, but it would not be enhanced by a special love of truth about the cleanliness level of the library floor. If I am a cleanliness fanatic, then given my argument in Chapter One, I have a reason to be conscientious about my beliefs about cleanliness, but my peculiarity does not give me knowledge or enhance the epistemic status of my belief. What does give me knowledge, according to the conscientiousness theory, is getting the truth out of a general love of truth and the virtues I develop from caring about truth. Nonetheless, we are still forced to the conclusion that knowledge in a given case is not very valuable if the truth it enhances is not desirable.

This is a general problem about the value of knowledge, no matter what account of knowledge we prefer. In every definition we have considered in this book, even when the definition succeeds at identifying a feature of the belief state that makes it better than mere true belief, if truly believing some proposition is not especially good, knowing the same proposition is not especially good either, and the situation is not improved by insisting that every true belief has some value simply in virtue of being true. There is no reason to think that the value of truth in itself is very great, and whatever value it has, it can be outweighed by other features of a belief that make it undesirable all things considered.

I do not see this as an objection to any of our accounts of knowledge. The problem is not with the definitions, but with our interest in knowledge. Knowledge has received sustained attention throughout the history of philosophy largely because we assume that knowledge is a great good, important enough to be worth all that attention. But upon reflection, it appears that not every instance of knowledge is especially valuable. But surely *some* knowledge is highly desirable, and it is because of the instances of knowledge that are highly desirable that we devote a lot of time to investigating knowledge in general.

What this means, I think, is that it is important for epistemologists to focus on *desirable truths*, not simply truths. To explain what makes a truth desirable, we can go back to what we care about individually or collectively, and that gets us a certain distance toward answering this question. We care about many things individually, and collectively we care about morality and such things as collective safety. What we individually and collectively care about upon reflection is no doubt in the domain of things we trust. Since self-trust commits us to trust in others, what we care about is subject to checks by other people we trust. If I am obsessed with the number of grains of sand on the beach and other people tell me that is a bizarre thing to care about, I probably should listen to them (unless I am Archimedes).

The issue of the limits of what we should individually and collectively care about is not a subject for epistemology, but it affects the way we think about epistemological questions. The fact that there is a distinction between desirable and undesirable truths leads to a distinction between desirable knowledge and trivial or undesirable knowledge. If we want a good life, we want a significant amount of desirable knowledge. We might even want to minimize undesirable knowledge, but I suspect that we don't need to make a special effort to do the latter.

We have already looked at cases in which the agent gets credit for the truth when the truth is not desirable. There are also cases in which she gets credit for the truth when the truth is desirable, but she does not get credit for the desirability of the truth. In other words, it may be a matter of luck that she gets a desirable truth even though it is not luck that she got a truth. It sometimes happens in scientific investigation that a researcher makes an important discovery by luck. In some of these cases, it is not luck that the researcher found out something true, but it is luck that the discovery turned out to be important.

Does a believer get more epistemic credit if she is credited with getting a desirable truth than if she is merely credited with getting the truth? I have suggested that she does (Zagzebski, 2003b). If it is not accidental that she learns something desirable as well as something true, she has a higher kind of knowledge than if she gets the truth non-accidentally, but it is accidental that the truth she gets is a desirable one. The agent is in an epistemically superior state when she is aware of the desirability of the truth she pursues. Someone who accidentally discovers a truth is like Columbus who accidentally discovered America while searching for another land using erroneous calculations. Someone who is credited with getting the truth but accidentally gets a desirable truth is like Columbus would have been if he had aimed for an unknown body of land with correct calculations on how to get there. Someone who is credited with both getting the truth and getting a desirable truth is like Columbus would have been if he had had reason for believing he was headed for a major continent and used the right calculations in doing so.

Of course, epistemic credit for getting a desirable truth is only one kind of credit. It is also important that we do something with the desirable truths we acquire to make our lives and the lives of others better.

In Chapter One I argued that the more we care about a domain, the more conscientious we ought to be in obtaining beliefs in that domain. But unfortunately, some of the most important truths are hard to learn, so even the highly conscientious believer may get only modest results. Aristotle makes a fascinating comment related to this that I think would change the way we conduct intellectual inquiry if we took it seriously. He says that even meager knowledge of celestial things is more pleasureful than all our knowledge of the world we live in, just as a half glimpse of a person we love is more delightful than a clear and complete view of other things (*Parts of Animals* 644b32–35). Contemporary epistemologists' examples of knowledge are states whose object is clear, simple, uncontroversial, and accessible to any-body, and the focus of theoretical attention is on the *way* in which we come to grasp the object of belief or the grounds for the belief, not the object itself. So the simplest cases of knowledge by perception or memory are the paradigm. These cases are the least demanding on the knower as an agent, and they make few demands on the theory that attempts to explain them.

But once we consider potential knowledge of what Aristotle calls celestial things, matters look different. The importance of the object makes the state of grasping the object valuable, even if the way in which the object is grasped is defective. In other words, as long as we get an important truth, we might not care if we get *credit* for reaching the truth. That means it might be better to merely believe something true and important than to know a more mundane matter.

Most of our attention in Chapter Five was on the difference between knowing and truly believing the same thing. If we paid more attention to the difference in the value of epistemic objects, it would not be so crucial to compare different ways of coming to believe the ordinary. We would be more interested in getting the right object than the right method of reaching the object.

The usual method of investigating knowledge is distorted in another way too because the nature of the object of knowledge might dictate the appropriate way of coming to know it. When the object is out of the ordinary, our way of coming to know it is probably also out of the ordinary. Ironically, we would not be doing epistemology at all if we were not interested in finding out how to know the things that are most important, but an investigation of empirical knowledge is probably not going to tell us much about that.

I think this is one of the reasons the epistemology of religion is so difficult. The models in general use in epistemology are usually inappropriate for the domain of religion. The same point applies to the domain of philosophy. How should a conscientious believer acquire philosophical beliefs? If there is philosophical knowledge, what theory of knowledge would account for it? I seriously doubt that we will find out by examining knowledge of perceptual objects, much less by comparing the difference between knowing and truly believing propositions about those objects.

My position is that we acquire the higher kinds of knowledge by imitating those who have it, the people we consider wise. I do not mean that we believe what they believe on their testimony, but rather that we learn how to acquire knowledge of the kinds of things they know by imitating their intellectual habits and ways of knowing. This requires trust in our ability to identify people with wisdom, as well as trust in their superior ability to acquire the most desirable kinds of knowledge. I think we do the same thing when we acquire knowledge in specialized fields: We imitate those who have mastered the field. Ways of knowing that rely only upon our own natural faculties and do not involve imitation of others are limited to very basic knowledge, what I have called "easy knowledge." Even though love of truth, like sympathy for the well-being of others, is natural, the disciplined love of truth I have called conscientiousness is learned from others.

Most of what an epistemically conscientious person does is picked up from exemplars, and I think that intellectual virtues are learned by imitation in a way that parallels the learning of the moral virtues. Learning by imitation is obvious in specialized fields such as anthropology, medicine, architecture, and gardening. There are methods developed by practitioners of each field that are transmitted to the next generation during the course of the practice of the field. The same point applies to methods of meditation and contemplation developed over many centuries by spiritually wise mentors in religious communities. With luck, imitating an exemplar of spiritual wisdom can result in high-grade knowledge, or perhaps it results in understanding, the topic of the next section.

II. UNDERSTANDING

Epistemology has been dominated by the values of certainty and understanding at different times in the history of philosophy, and the difference was reflected in the way knowledge was understood. As a rough generalization, the dominant value was certainty in eras marked by the fear of skepticism, and in those periods knowledge was closely associated with justification, since justification is what we want to defend our right to be sure. In contrast, understanding was the dominant value in those eras in which skepticism was not seen as threatening. Knowledge at those times was closely associated with explanation, since understanding is exhibited by giving an explanation.

As we saw in Chapters Two and Three, skepticism has had an enormous impact on modern philosophy, so it is not surprising that understanding has received little attention. One of the sad consequences of neglect of a value is fragmentation of meaning. People can mean so many different things by the word "understanding" that it is hard to identify the state that has been ignored. This can generate a vicious circle since neglect leads to fragmentation of meaning, which seems to justify further neglect and further fragmentation until eventually a concept can disappear entirely.[5]

Fortunately, there are signs that the neglect of understanding is being remedied.[6] In this section I want to draw attention to some interesting features of understanding, and will consider some of the ways in which understanding is good for us, perhaps better for us, in general, than knowledge.

Some philosophers think that understanding is a form of knowledge (Grimm, 2006), and perhaps they are right, but I want to stress the differences between propositional knowledge and a kind of understanding that is both important and neglected. In fact, I find it doubtful that understanding in the sense I have in mind is directed at propositions at all. To take a simple example, when we get understanding from a map or a graph, do we grasp propositions? Maps, graphs, and diagrams are nonpropositional representations of something—for example, the layout of a city, the relationship between interest rates and the rate of inflation, the connection between Plato's world of Forms and the physical world, and so on. I do not deny that when someone understands something nonpropositionally there is often a propositional alternative to the nonpropositional representation. If you can explain propositionally how to get from one part of a city to another, we might think that is just as good as seeing how to get there on a map. The same point applies to explaining propositionally how one economic factor varies with another, or the relationship between Plato's two worlds. After all, *Plato* explained his theory propositionally. But it doesn't follow from that that the state of understanding something via a graph or diagram is the same state as grasping or believing a set of propositions.

It is possible that *what* is understood nonpropositionally (e.g., the layout of a city) is the same part of concrete reality as what can be known propositionally. Maybe understanding and propositional knowledge are different ways of cognitively grasping the same thing. I suspect that that is true, but I also think that understanding is not just a different route to the same end. In some cases, propositional

---

[5] I think the terms "virtue" and "vice" were victims of this cycle of neglect and fragmentation until virtue ethics made a comeback a generation ago.

[6] Some recent work on understanding appears in Kvanvig (2003), Riggs (2003), and Grimm (2005).

knowledge is a meager substitute for understanding—for instance, understanding a person you love. Consider also what it means to understand a work of art or music. I have a distinguished elderly friend who used to be highly musical and regularly read music scores for entertainment. He recently complained to me that he lost the ability to listen to music. He can still hear the music—that is, he can hear the sounds, but he cannot understand it anymore. What is it that he used to be able to do and no longer can? Even if it is possible to describe musical structures propositionally, I find it doubtful that a grasp of those propositions is what he lost, and it is also doubtful that a grasp of certain propositions would be an adequate substitute for what he used to be able to do while listening to music.

I have proposed that knowledge was closely connected with understanding in askeptical periods of philosophical history, but I only want to mention Plato as an example. Plato closely connected *epistêmê* (knowledge) with understanding.[7] Some Plato scholars have argued that *epistêmê* in Plato is associated with the mastery of a *technê*—a practical human art or skill.[8] Plato's idea of *technai* include such complex activities as medicine, hunting, and ship-building, as well as more specific practical skills such as cooking, or even pastry-making. Modern examples would include football, archaeology, and playing the cello. The person who has mastered a *technê* has a kind of understanding one cannot get any other way. He is able to explain features of the *technê* and to answer questions related to its practice. Gail Fine says:

> On the account [of Plato] I have proposed, one knows more to the extent that one can explain more; knowledge requires, not a vision, and not some special sort of certainty or infallibility, but sufficiently rich, mutually supporting, explanatory accounts. Knowledge, for Plato, does not proceed piecemeal; to know, one must master a whole field, by interrelating and explaining its diverse elements. (1990, p. 114)

According to Fine, to have *epistêmê* in Plato's sense, one must have mastered an entire field. One does not have *epistêmê* of an

---

[7] Moravcsik (1979) translates *"epistêmê"* as "understanding," whereas Gail Fine (1990) translates it "knowledge," but stresses that it is a form of knowledge that is closely connected to understanding.

[8] See Moravcsik (1979), Fine (1990), Woodruff (1990), and Benson (2000), sec. 9.4.

astronomical fact without interrelating and explaining its relation to diverse elements within the field of astronomy, and one can do that only by mastering the *technê* of being an astronomer. So one does not understand a part of a field without the ability to explain its place within a much larger theoretical framework, and one acquires the ability to do that by mastering a skill. Likewise, one does not have *epistêmê* of some feature of human psychology without the ability to explain how that feature fits into the larger framework of human psychology, and that requires having mastered the *technê* of the psychologist.

Julius Moravcsik also argues that understanding was Plato's central epistemological aim and he contrasts that with propositional knowledge:

> The only propositional knowledge that will be of interest will be that which is derived from the kind of theoretical understanding that Plato envisages. Mere knowledge of truths is of no interest to Plato; propositional knowledge figures in the dialogues only insofar as this may be, in some contexts, evidence for understanding, and needed for practical activity. (1979, p. 60)

Of course, Plato has a lot more to say about *epistêmê*, but I have chosen these comments about his epistemology because I think they bring out two points that are applicable to a contemporary investigation of understanding. One is that understanding is connected with learning an art or skill, a *technê*. One gains understanding by knowing how to do something well, and this makes one a reliable person to consult in matters pertaining to the skill in question. I do not clam that every instance of understanding is connected with a *technê* in this way. Some instances of understanding are so easy that they require nothing more than simple past experience—for example, understanding a stop sign in the United States. So I think there are probably cases of "easy understanding," just as there are cases of "easy knowledge." But I am suggesting that the more interesting and significant examples of understanding are connected with skills.

This leads to the second idea, which is that understanding is not directed toward a discrete proposition, but involves grasping relations of parts to other parts and perhaps the relation of parts to a whole. Relations can be spatial, such as the relative location of sites in a city, and they can be temporal, as in a musical composition. An important kind of relation is that of cause to effect, or more generally, what

Stephen Grimm (2005) calls dependency relations. Grimm proposes that understanding is fundamentally the grasp of dependency relations. It seems to me that one's mental representation of the relations one grasps can be mediated by maps, graphs, diagrams, and three-dimensional models in addition to, or even in place of, the acceptance of a series of propositions.

There is a third feature of understanding that distinguishes it from propositional knowledge and which has some interesting implications: Knowledge can be acquired by testimony, whereas understanding cannot be. A conscientious believer can obtain a true belief on the testimony of another, and given the right conditions, can thereby acquire knowledge. Of course, there are numerous issues about the conditions under which a belief acquired by testimony constitutes knowledge, but practically nobody denies that testimonial knowledge is possible. A state of knowing can be conveyed from one person to another because knowing is a form of believing and belief can be conveyed from one person to another.[9]

Understanding cannot be transmitted in that way. In fact, understanding cannot be given to another person at all except in the indirect sense that a good teacher can sometimes recreate the conditions that produce understanding in hopes that the student will acquire it also. So if you understand how to get from the Duomo to the Uffizi in Florence by looking at a map, you can give someone else the same understanding by handing them the map and tracing the route with your finger. You can also draw diagrams and graphs, and you can play a passage of music over and over, exaggerating the patterns. But in those cases in which understanding requires the mastery of a *techné*, you cannot give someone understanding without teaching them the *techné*. Someone can learn auto mechanics or cooking or fly fishing or philosophy from another person, but they cannot acquire understanding by testimony. If my colleague believes that the leaves on his maple tree are turning bright red, he can tell me, and if I trust him, I may believe it too, and if he knows the leaves are red, I may also know it, assuming the two of us satisfy whatever conditions your theory of knowledge requires. But there is no analogous way in which he can transmit his understanding of trees to me. Unlike beliefs, understanding is not passed along from a

---

[9] Stephen Grimm has pointed out to me that not every form of propositional knowledge can be transmitted through testimony, for example, knowledge *a priori*. I can know by testimony what somebody else knows *a priori*, but then I don't know it *a priori*. Another possible exception is moral knowledge, which we will discuss below.

testifier to a recipient. The person's own mind has to do the "work" of understanding.

I think this is important in solving a puzzle about moral knowledge. Some philosophers think there is something epistemically or morally deficient about a person who accepts moral beliefs on testimony.[10] A conscientious person allegedly comes to her moral beliefs by using her own moral sense and background knowledge, and accepts no moral belief on the testimony of another person. There are no moral authorities.

This view is widespread, but it is hard to see how it can be defended. Clearly, a child in need of moral education may rightly acquire moral beliefs from trusted adults, and even adults may rightly find many moral issues too complicated to figure out for themselves, and may justifiably rely upon those whom they trust for the answer to questions of moral judgment. Reliance upon trusted others is common in judgments about issues in bio-ethics, environmental ethics, and professional ethics, since these cases often depend in part upon nonmoral knowledge in specialized fields. A harder case is one in which a normal adult is capable of making an informed moral judgment about some issue and no specialized non-moral knowledge that the agent lacks is required to make the judgment, so while she *could* come to a moral judgment on her own without relying upon testimony, she chooses not to.

Let's suppose that S accepts the moral judgment of A on the assumption that if A has satisfied the requirements for knowing whether a certain action is right or wrong, it is not necessary for her to do the same thing. S might either judge that A is a person with superior practical wisdom and is a better moral judge of the matter than she is herself, and she trusts that judgment, or she might simply trust her judgment that A is at least equal to herself in practical wisdom and any necessary background knowledge. Since we do not normally think it is illegitimate for S to accept a belief on the testimony of A even when S could, in principle, get the information firsthand, why should we think that the situation is any different when a moral issue is involved? If epistemic egoism is mistaken (and, if I was right in Chapter Four, inconsistent), why would moral epistemic egoism be any better?

---

[10] See Robert Hopkins (2007) for an interesting discussion of this problem. Hopkins argues that there is no reason to deny that moral testimony makes knowledge available to the recipient. If there is a problem with accepting moral beliefs on testimony, it must be that there is some norm that makes the knowledge unusable. Hopkins suggests that the most likely candidate for such a norm is the requirement that we grasp for ourselves the moral reasons behind a moral view.

In arguing for the incoherence of epistemic egoism, I claimed that to the extent that I have evidence that I am more trustworthy than some others, I also have evidence that some others are more trustworthy than I am. Furthermore, my emotion of epistemic admiration is in the circle of features of myself that I must trust in advance of the evidence of my trustworthiness. Both reasons can lead me to reasonably trust the moral judgment of another person at least as much as I trust my own. Of course, there is a trivial sense in which I must follow my conscience—If my belief leads to action, I am the one who makes the final judgment upon which I act. But that does not mean that I should follow unaided conscience. As Elizabeth Anscombe (1981) argued a quarter century ago, only a foolish person thinks that his own conscience is the last word. "Just as any reasonable man knows that his memory may sometimes deceive him, any reasonable man knows that what one has conscientiously decided one may later conscientiously regret" (p. 46). A conscientious person forestalls later conscientious regret by consulting others whom he admires for their wisdom in the matter at issue, or whom his evidence indicates are trustworthy in the particular case.

For these reasons, it seems to me that I can have a moral belief based on testimony that is epistemically conscientious, and if it is epistemically conscientious, I have an epistemic right to believe it. Furthermore, if such a belief is true, it can constitute knowledge. I do not see anything epistemically wrong, in principle, with moral beliefs on the word of another, so if there is anything wrong with such beliefs, it would have to be a moral reason, not an epistemic one. Perhaps there is such a reason, and if so, it is something that would have to be treated in a work of ethics, not epistemology.

Notice, however, that we have identified an epistemic good that testimony cannot give us, and that is understanding. If my union calls a strike, I may be within my epistemic rights in believing that I should strike, based on the testimony of trusted others, and I may be within my rights in acting upon that belief, but if I do not grasp the moral reasons for striking, I lack an important epistemic good. If my Church teaches that abortion is wrong, I may be within my epistemic rights in believing that it is wrong, but if I do not grasp the reasons for the wrongness, I am in an epistemic position inferior to the one I would be in if I did grasp the reasons. But this does not show anything peculiar to moral testimony, since I have argued that testimony in general cannot give us understanding.

Why is moral understanding important? One reason is that moral understanding allows us to see connections among individual moral judgments, so if we adopt a moral belief on testimony without understanding the broader moral reasons behind it, we will be unable to generalize our judgment to make relevantly similar judgments. For instance, if I believe that a certain act is sexist on the testimony of another, a lack of understanding of the way in which the act is sexist and the principles that make sexism wrong prevents me from using that knowledge to make judgments on the wrongness of other acts. A lack of understanding also prevents me from being able to critically reflect on ways that some of my other judgments ought to be revised in light of the judgment of the wrongness of the sexist act.[11]

Moral understanding is generally important to a good life, but it does not follow that I am lacking anything of importance if I do not understand the moral reasons for each and every moral belief I have. For instance, I do not think it is important that everyone understands the moral reasons for the belief that wantonly producing greenhouse gases without regard to the environment is immoral. If my elderly neighbor accepts that belief on testimony, he lacks understanding of the moral issue and so he lacks an epistemic good he might have had, but it is not very important either for his life or for the life of others that he have that understanding. None of us can understand everything, not even everything of moral significance, and part of the trust we need to live good lives is trust that others in our community have the understanding we lack. There is probably some moral understanding that everyone lacks, and it aids our lives if we can identify those areas as well.

Why is moral understanding in general more important than understanding about other domains? I think that the answer is the Platonic one that living a life is a *technê;* life is a practical domain, and living well is mastering the *technê* of living. Moral understanding is related to living well as understanding medicine is related to being a good physician, and understanding auto mechanics is related to being a good auto mechanic. Since no one else can live our lives for us, we each need the understanding necessary to mastering the *technê* of living our lives.

But we do not invent the *technê* of our lives from the ground up. There is a community of collective skills the learning of which makes it possible for the individuals in the community to live lives that include caring about the many optional things we care about. Moral

---

[11] Both of these reasons are mentioned by Karen Jones (1999).

understanding arises from learning the skills of living in a community. To master the *technê* of living our individual lives, we also need understanding of the other domains we care about. Understanding is not just something that makes our lives more desirable than they would be otherwise; understanding of morality and the other domains we care about is essential to mastering the *technê* of living our lives.[12]

I have said nothing in this book about whether we can choose what we care about in optional domains and if so, how we decide what to care about. This question takes us back to the nature of the self and leads directly into an issue that I have avoided in this book because of its difficulty: self-knowledge and self-understanding.[13] It seems to me very improbable that there are no norms for optional caring. To care about things at whim is no doubt unwise, but there is no reason to think that there are rules that tell me what I should care about in optional domains. If there were, the caring would not really be optional.

To a great extent we define ourselves by what we care about, so we have to be careful what we care about; we might not like what we become by caring about a certain thing. But why would we not like it if we really become what we care about? For instance, if we define ourselves by caring about how we look, why would we not like being the kind of person who cares so much about his or her looks? I suspect that the answer is that there are undiscovered parts of the self that are revealed when we act against those parts, and those parts are not chosen. Or if they are chosen, they were chosen a long time in the past. This is one of the many ways understanding the self is a condition for happiness.

III. THE INTELLECT AND THE HIGHEST GOOD

I find it fascinating that many major philosophers in the West thought that the highest good is a state of the intellect. Since one of the themes of this book is the issue of what makes knowledge good, I think it is appropriate to end the book by noting the curious fact that

---

[12] For an insightful paper on the relationship between moral skill and moral authority, see W. H. Walsh (1965).

[13] See Stephen Hetherington (2007) for a nicely written, accessible book on knowing the self and what persons are.

for some philosophers, knowledge is not good simply because it serves some other good; a special type of knowledge *is* the good for which we ultimately strive.

In Plato's *Symposium* (206a) Socrates says in his speech in praise of love that love is the desire for the perpetual possession of Beauty. Possession takes place in a cognitive act, in the apprehension of the eternal Forms, the highest human achievement. In Book X of the *Nicomachean Ethics*, Aristotle argues that happiness is an activity in accordance with virtue, and the highest human activity is contemplation of truth. He gives two reasons for that. One is that the intellect is the best element in us; the other is that the objects of the intellect are the best of the things that can be known (1177a19–21). He goes on to say that the activity of contemplation is more pleasureful than any other, including inquiry: "For philosophy or the pursuit of wisdom offers pleasures marvelous both in purity and permanence; and it is reasonable that those who have attained the truth will spend their life more pleasantly than those who are occupied in pursuing the truth" (1177a25–27).

Aquinas adds a supernatural layer to Aristotle's view of happiness. Happiness is a state of satiation of the will. The happy person has the whole good; there is nothing left to will. The will wills to possess, and reality is possessed in contemplation. All of reality is grasped in the Beatific Vision, the state of the blessed in heaven who know all of reality through their vision of God.[14] Happiness is only fully attainable in the afterlife, but it is interesting that even in heaven, the will is fully satisfied in an intellectual state.

Spinoza is perhaps the most highly original of all philosophers in that his work is most unlike the work of any other philosopher. But Spinoza agrees with many of the other important philosophers of the West that the culmination of human endeavor is an intellectual state. Spinoza distinguishes three levels of knowledge. The lowest level is *imagination*, by which we get the data of the senses. This data is the correlate in thought of states of the body as it is randomly affected by the bodies around it. Imagination is superficial, haphazard, relative to the perceiver, and the source of much error. There is no knowledge of essences at this level, nor knowledge of necessary causal connections. The second level is *ratio*, or scientific knowledge, by which a person is able to grasp the essences of objects. Through reason a

---

[14] See Aquinas's *Treatise on Happiness, Summa Theologica* I–II, qq. 1–5, published separately in Aquinas and Oesterle (1983), and the Thomistically inspired work by Josef Pieper (1998).

person apprehends the mathematical laws of nature and their expression in the causal dependencies of one part of nature on another. As I interpret Spinoza, *ratio* is a form of understanding in the sense I described in the last section. The third and highest level of knowledge is *scientia intuitiva*, or intuitive knowledge. At this level a person is able to grasp each thing in the universe in the context of an infinite explanatory system, *Deus sive natura*. Nature *is* God and it is infinite, so the world in its entirety cannot be grasped in its details, but it can be intuited in a single grasp of mind. No human being can achieve this fully since to have it, one would have to have an infinite mind, the mind of God, but humans can approach it asymptotically. In intuitive knowledge one sees the whole universe as a unity, so this also is a form of understanding.[15]

The highest state achievable for a human being is *amor dei intellectualis*, the intellectual love of God, which is both a state of emotional ecstasy and the cognitive state of intuitive knowledge. According to Spinoza, knowledge of God (= Nature) is the mind's greatest good, and indeed, the highest good of the human person.

I find it interesting that in philosophers otherwise as diverse as the two most important ancient Greek philosophers, the medieval Christian Aquinas, and Spinoza the early modern Jew, what we ultimately aim for is an intellectual state. Many philosophers believe that epistemology became a core area of philosophy because of Descartes, and I would not deny that Descartes gets the credit for a methodology of philosophy that starts with epistemology. But I think there is another, more ancient reason why epistemology is so important. If our ultimate happiness resides in a state of the intellect, it is important that we figure out how to attain it. There has always been a commitment to figuring that out, but before the modern period, philosophers approached the question of the nature of the highest state of the intellect via a study of human nature and the place of human beings in the universe. Knowledge was a crucial object of study, but it was considered a derivative object. After Descartes, knowledge became a primary object of study, by which I mean that it became an object of

---

[15] For a fascinating personal treatment of Spinoza the philosopher and the man, see Rebecca Goldstein (2006). Goldstein calls Spinoza's system "ecstatic rationalism." She shows how Spinoza shunned what most of us call the personal, yet he argued that the self expands in the intellectual love of God, the comprehension of the entire geometrically deduced system of nature he presents in his *Ethics*. The impersonal is the personal properly understood. Goldstein disagrees, proposing a way to understand Spinoza and his philosophy that he would not have condoned, but in doing so, she makes him very appealing.

study in advance of a study of the world in which knowledge occurs, and prior to the investigation of the kind of being that is a knower. But nobody would care about adopting that methodology unless they were already convinced that knowledge is important, or if not knowledge, then some other state of intellect.

I think it is because we care about knowledge so much that we care about investigating knowledge by whatever method we prefer. Descartes changed philosophy because he proposed a new method to inquire about something that philosophers have always deeply cared about. Ironically, the kind of knowledge that has historically been valued above all others gets virtually no attention in these naturalistic times, yet it is doubtful that epistemology would have evolved into the center of philosophy were it not for the aspiration to the kind of knowledge that is neglected.

FURTHER READING

Renewed interest in epistemic value arose out of the recent work in virtue epistemology. For some overviews of this development, see Duncan Pritchard, "Recent Work on Epistemic Value," *American Philosophical Quarterly* 44 (2007, 85–110), and Wayne Riggs, "The Value Turn in Epistemology," in Vincent Hendricks and Duncan Pritchard (eds.), *New Waves in Epistemology* (Palgrave Macmillan, 2008). For an excellent book on the variety of epistemic values, see William Alston's *Beyond "Justification": Dimensions of Epistemic Evaluation* (Ithaca, NY: Cornell University Press, 2006). Timothy Chappell's *Values and Virtues: Aristotelianism in Contemporary Ethics* (Oxford: Oxford University Press, 2006) includes several fascinating papers on value. Students interested in issues in epistemic normativity may want to read several of the essays contained in Matthias Steup (ed.), *Knowledge, Truth, and Duty: Essays on Epistemic Justification, Responsibility, and Virtue* (Oxford: Oxford University Press, 2001). More advanced students may want to take a look at Kvanvig's fascinating account of understanding which can be found in his last chapter "Knowledge and Understanding" in Jonathan L. Kvanvig, *The Value of Knowledge and the Pursuit of Understanding* (Cambridge: Cambridge University Press, 2003). For students interested in the latest direction epistemological discourse is turning, see Stephen Hetherington, *Epistemology Futures* (Oxford: Oxford University Press, 2006).

Bibliography

Aikin, Scott (2005), "Who's afraid of epistemology's regress problem?" *Philosophical Studies*, 126:2.

Allison, S. T., Mackie, D. M., Muller, M. M., and Worth, L. T. (1993), "Sequential correspondence biases and perceptions of change: The Castro studies revisited," *Personality and Social Psychology Bulletin* 19, 151–57.

Alston, William P. (1991), *Perceiving God: the epistemology of religious experience* (Ithaca, NY: Cornell University Press).

Ambrose, Alice (1989), "Moore and Wittgenstein as teachers," *Teaching Philosophy* 12, 107–108.

Anscombe, G. E. M. (1981), *The collected philosophical papers of G.E.M. Anscombe*, 3 vols. (Minneapolis: University of Minnesota Press).

Aquinas, Thomas and Oesterle, John A. (1983), *Treatise on happiness* (Notre Dame, IN: University of Notre Dame Press).

Aristocles and Chiesara, Maria Lorenza (2001), *Aristocles of Messene: testimonia and fragments* (Oxford;New York: Oxford University Press).

Augustine, Mourant, John A. and Collinge, William J. (1992), *Four anti-Pelagian writings* (Washington, DC: Catholic University of America Press).

Axtell, Guy (2000), *Knowledge, belief, and character: readings in virtue epistemology* (Lanham, MD: Rowman & Littlefield).

Bell, B. E. and Loftus, Elizabeth F. (1989), "Trivial persuasion in the courtroom: The power of (a few) minor details," *Journal of Personality and Social Psychology* 56, 669–79.

Benson, Hugh H. (2000), *Socratic wisdom: the model of knowledge in Plato's early dialogues* (New York: Oxford University Press).

Blackburn, Simon (2005), *Truth: a guide* (Oxford;New York: Oxford University Press).

Block, J. and Funder, D. C. (1986), "Social roles and social perception: Individual differences in attribution and error." *Journal of Personality and Social Psychology* 51, 1200–1207.

Boghossian, Paul (1997), "What the externalist can know a priori," *Proceedings of the Aristotelian Society* 97, 161–75.

BonJour, Laurence (1976), "The coherence theory of empirical knowledge," *Philosophical Studies* 30, 281–312.

———— (1978), "Can empirical knowledge have a foundation?" *American Philosophical Quarterly* 15:1, 1–13.

———— (1985), *The structure of empirical knowledge* (Cambridge, MA: Harvard University Press).

BonJour, Laurence and Sosa, Ernest (2003), *Epistemic justification: internalism vs. externalism, foundations vs. virtues* (Malden, MA: Blackwell).

Bouwsma, O. K. (1965), *Philosophical essays* (Lincoln: University of Nebraska Press).

Bregman, N. J. and McAllister, H. A. (1982), "Eyewitness testimony: The role of commitment in increasing reliability," *Social Psychology Quarterly* 45, 181–84.

Brueckner, Anthony (1992), "Semantic answers to skepticism," *Pacific Philosophical Quarterly* 73, 200–19.

Buckhout, Robert (1974), "Eyewitness testimony," *Scientific American* December, 23–31.

Burge, Tyler (1979), "Individualism and the mental," *Midwest Studies in Philosophy* IV, 73–121.

———— (1988), "Individualism and self-knowledge," *Journal of Philosophy* 85, 649–63.

Chappell, Timothy (2006), *Values and virtues: Aristotelianism in contemporary ethics* (Oxford;New York: Oxford University Press).

Chisholm, Roderick M. (1964), *Theory of knowledge* (Englewood Cliffs, NJ: Prentice Hall).

———— (1977), *Theory of knowledge* (2nd ed.; Englewood Cliffs, NJ: Prentice Hall).

———— (1982), *The foundations of knowing* (Minneapolis: University of Minnesota Press).

Churchland, Paul M. (1988), *Matter and consciousness: a contemporary introduction to the philosophy of mind* (Cambridge, MA: MIT Press).

Clifford, William Kingdon, Stephen, Leslie, and Pollock, Frederick (1901), *Lectures and essays by the late William Kingdon Clifford, F.R.S* (London; New York: Macmillan).

Cutler, Brian L. and Penrod, Steven (1995), *Mistaken identification: the eyewitness, psychology, and the law* (Cambridge;New York: Cambridge University Press).

Dennett, Daniel (1987), *The intentional stance* (Cambridge, MA: MIT Press).

DePaul, Michael (1993), *Balance and refinement: beyond coherence methods of moral inquiry* (London;New York: Routledge).

——— (2001a), *Resurrecting old-fashioned foundationalism* (Lanham, MD: Rowman & Littlefield).

——— (2001b), "Value monism in epistemology," in Matthias Steup (ed.), *Knowledge, truth, and duty: essays on epistemic justification, virtue, and responsibility* (Oxford;New York: Oxford University Press).

DePaul, Michael and Zagzebski, Linda (2003), *Intellectual virtue: perspectives from ethics and epistemology* (Oxford: Clarendon Press).

DeRose, Keith (1995), "Solving the skeptical problem," *Philosophical Review* 104:1, 1–52.

DeRose, Keith and Warfield, Ted A. (1999), *Skepticism: a contemporary reader* (New York: Oxford University Press).

Descartes, René (1984), *The philosophical writings of Descartes*, 3 vols. (Cambridge;New York: Cambridge University Press).

Dewey, John (1933), *How we think, a restatement of the relation of reflective thinking to the educative process* (Boston;New York: D.C. Heath and Company).

Dretske, Fred (1970), "Epistemic operators," *Journal of Philosophy* 67, 1007–23.

——— (1971), "Conclusive reasons," *Australasian Journal of Philosophy* 49, 1–22.

——— (1995), *Naturalizing the mind* (Cambridge, MA: MIT Press).

Emerson, Ralph Waldo and Mumford, Lewis (1968), *Essays and journals* (Garden City, NY: International Collectors Library).

Fairweather, Abrol and Zagzebski, Linda (2001), *Virtue epistemology: essays on epistemic virtue and responsibility* (Oxford;New York: Oxford University Press).

Fantl, Jeremy (2003), "Modest infinitism," *Canadian Journal of Philosophy* 33:4.

Feldman, Richard (2003), *Epistemology* (Upper Saddle River, NJ: Prentice Hall).

Fine, Gail (1990), "Knowledge and belief in *Republic* v–vii," in Stephen Everson (ed.), *Epistemology (Companions to Ancient Thought: 1)* (Cambridge: Cambridge University Press), 85–115.

Foley, Richard (2001), *Intellectual trust in oneself and others* (Cambridge;New York: Cambridge University Press).

Frankfurt, Harry G. (2005), *On bullshit* (Princeton, NJ: Princeton University Press).

Fricker, Elizabeth (2006), "Testimony and epistemic autonomy," in Jennifer Lackey and Ernest Sosa (eds.), *The epistemology of testimony* (Oxford: Clarendon Press).

Fricker, Miranda (2007), *Epistemic injustice: power and the ethics of knowing* (Oxford;New York: Oxford University Press).

Fumerton, Richard (2001), "Classical foundationalism," in Michael DePaul (ed.), *Resurrecting old-fashioned foundationalism* (Lanham, MD: Rowman & Littlefield), 3–20.

Gettier, Edmund L. (1963), "Is justified true belief knowledge?" *Analysis* 23, 121–23.

Goldman, Alvin I. (1979), "What is justified belief?" in George S. Pappas (ed.), *Justification and knowledge: new studies in epistemology* (Boston: D. Reidel), 1–23.

Goldstein, Rebecca (2006), *Betraying Spinoza: the renegade Jew who gave us modernity* (New York: Nextbook:Schocken).

Greco, John (1999), "Agent reliabilism," *Philosophical Perspectives* 13, 273–96.

——— (2003), "Knowledge as credit for true belief," in Michael DePaul and Linda Zagzebski (eds.), *Intellectual virtue* (Oxford: Oxford University Press).

——— (2004), *Ernest Sosa and his critics* (Malden, MA: Blackwell).

Grimm, Stephen R. (2005), "Understanding as an epistemic goal," Dissertation (University of Notre Dame).

——— (2006), "Is understanding a species of knowledge?" *British Journal for the Philosophy of Science* 57, 515–35.

Haack, Susan (1993), *Evidence and inquiry: towards reconstruction in epistemology* (Oxford;Cambridge: Blackwell).

Hawthorne, John (2004), *Knowledge and lotteries* (Oxford;New York: Oxford University Press).

Heil, John (1988), "Privileged access," *Mind* 97, 238–51.

Hetherington, Stephen Cade (2001), *Good knowledge, bad knowledge: on two dogmas of epistemology* (Oxford;New York: Oxford University Press).

——— (2006), *Epistemology futures* (Oxford;New York: Oxford University Press).

——— (2007), *Self-knowledge: beginning philosophy right here and now* (Orchard Park, NY: Broadview Press).

Hopkins, Robert (2007), "What is wrong with moral testimony," *Philosophy & Phenomenological Research* 74:3, 611–34.

Howard-Snyder, Daniel and Frances and Feit, Neil (2003), "Infallibilism and Gettier's legacy," *Philosophy & Phenomenological Research* 66:2, 304–27.

James, William (1979), *The will to believe and other essays in popular philosophy* (Cambridge, MA: Harvard University Press).

Jones, Karen (1999), "Second-hand moral knowledge," *Journal of Philosophy* 96:2, 55–78.

Kahneman, Daniel and Tversky, Amos (1979), "Intuitive prediction: Biases and corrective procedures," *Management Science* 12, 313–27.

Klein, Peter D. (1976), "Knowledge, causality, and defeasibility," *Journal of Philosophy* 73, 792–812.

———— (1999), "Human knowledge and the infinite regress of reasons," *Philosophical Perspectives* 13, 297–325.

———— (2000), "The failures of dogmatism and a new Pyrrhonism," *Acta Analytica: Philosophy and Psychology* 15:24, 7–24.

Kornblith, Hilary (1993), "Epistemic normativity," *Synthese* 94, 357–76.

Kripke, Saul A. (1980), *Naming and necessity* (Cambridge, MA: Harvard University Press).

Kvanvig, Jonathan L. (2003), *The value of knowledge and the pursuit of understanding* (Cambridge;New York: Cambridge University Press).

Lackey, Jennifer and Sosa, Ernest (2006), *The epistemology of testimony* (Oxford;New York: Oxford University Press).

Lehrer, Keith (1965), "Knowledge, truth and evidence," *Analysis* 25, 168–75.

———— (2000), *Theory of knowledge* (2nd ed.; Boulder, CO: Westview Press).

Lehrer, Keith and Paxson, Jr., Thomas (1969), "Knowledge: Undefeated justified true belief," *Journal of Philosophy* 66:8, 225–37.

Lewis, David (1996), "Elusive knowledge," *Australasian Journal of Philosophy* 74, 549–67.

Loftus, Elizabeth F. (1996), *Eyewitness testimony* (Cambridge, MA: Harvard University Press).

Lycan, William G. (2006), "On the Gettier problem problem," in Stephen Cade Hetherington (ed.), *Epistemology futures* (Oxford;New York: Oxford University Press).

Lynch, Michael P. (2004), *True to life: why truth matters* (Cambridge, MA: MIT Press).

———— (forthcoming), "The values of truth and the truth of values," in A. Haddock, A. Millar, and D. H. Pritchard (eds.), *Epistemic value* (Oxford: Oxford University Press).

McEwan, Ian (2002), *Atonement: a novel* (1st ed.; New York: N.A. Talese/ Doubleday).

McGrew, Timothy J. (1995), *The foundations of knowledge* (Lanham, MD: Littlefield Adams Books).

McGrew, Timothy J. and McGrew, Lydia (2006), *Internalism and epistemology: the architecture of reason* (London;New York: Routledge).

McKinsey, Michael (1991), "Anti-individualism and privileged access," *Analysis* 51, 9–16.

McLaughlin, Brian and Tye, Michael (1998), "Is content-externalism compatible with privileged access?" *Philosophical Review* 107:3, 349–80.

Montaigne, Michel de (1958), *Complete essays* (Stanford: Stanford University Press).

Moore, G. E. (1959), *Philosophical papers* (London;New York: Macmillan).

Moravcsik, Julius (1979), "Understanding and knowledge in Plato's philosophy," *Neue Hefte für Philosophie* 15/16, 53–69.

Myers, David G. (2005), *Social psychology* (8th ed.; Boston: McGraw-Hill).

Nagel, Thomas (1986), *The view from nowhere* (New York: Oxford University Press).

Nozick, Robert (1981), *Philosophical explanations* (Cambridge, MA: Harvard University Press).

Pappas, George Sotiros and Swain, Marshall (1978), *Essays on knowledge and justification* (Ithaca, NY: Cornell University Press).

Peirce, Charles (1868), "Some consequences of four incapacities," *Journal of Speculative Philosophy* 2, 140–57.

Pieper, Josef (1998), *Happiness and contemplation* (South Bend, IN: St. Augustine's Press).

Plantinga, Alvin (1984), "Advice to Christian philosophers," *Faith and Philosophy* 1, 3.

———— (1993), *Warrant and proper function* (New York: Oxford University Press).

———— (2000), *Warranted Christian belief* (New York: Oxford University Press).

Plantinga, Alvin and Wolterstorff, Nicholas (1983), *Faith and rationality: reason and belief in God* (Notre Dame: University of Notre Dame Press).

Plato, Cooper, John M., and Hutchinson, D. S. (1997), *Complete works* (Indianapolis, IN: Hackett).

Pojman, Louis P. (2002), *The theory of knowledge: classical and contemporary readings* (3rd ed.; Belmont, CA: Wadsworth).

Pollock, John (2001), "Nondoxastic foundationalism," in Michael DePaul (ed.), *Resurrecting old-fashioned foundationalism* (Lanham, MD: Rowman & Littlefield), 41–57.

Pritchard, Duncan (2005), *Epistemic luck* (New York: Oxford University Press).

———— (2007), "Recent work on epistemic value," *American Philosophical Quarterly* 44, 85–110.

Putnam, Hilary (1975), *Philosophical papers 2* (London;New York: Cambridge University Press).

———— (1981), *Reason, truth, and history* (Cambridge;New York: Cambridge University Press).

Quine, W. V. (1969), *Ontological relativity, and other essays* (New York: Columbia University Press).

Riggs, Wayne (1998), "What are the 'chances' of being justified?" *Monist* 81:3.

———— (2003), "Understanding 'virtue' and the virtue of understanding," in Michael DePaul and Linda Zagzebski (eds.), *Intellectual virtue: perspectives from ethics and epistemology* (Oxford;New York: Oxford University Press), 203–26.

———— (2007), "Why epistemologists are so down on their luck," *Synthese* 158:3, 329–44.

Roberts, Robert and Wood, W. Jay (2007), *Intellectual virtues: an essay in regulative epistemology* (Oxford;New York: Oxford University Press).

Rorty, Richard (1979), *Philosophy and the mirror of nature* (Princeton: Princeton University Press).

Ross, Lee (1977), "The intuitive psychologist and his shortcomings: Distortions in the attribution process," in L. Berkowitz (ed.), *Advances in experimental social psychology* (New York: Academic Press).

Ross, Lee and Anderson, Craig A. (1982), "Shortcomings in the attribution process: On the origins and maintenance of erroneous social assessments," in P. Slovic, D. Kahneman, and A. Tversky (eds.), *Judgment under uncertainty: heuristics and biases* (New York: Cambridge University Press).

Sartwell, Crispin (1992), "Why knowledge is merely true belief," *Journal of Philosophy* 89, 167–80.

Sosa, Ernest (1974), "How do you know?" *American Philosophical Quarterly* 11, 113–22.

———— (1991), *Knowledge in perspective* (New York: Cambridge University Press).

———— (1994a), "Philosophical scepticism, I," *Aristotelian Society* 68, 263–90.

———— (1994b), "Virtue perspectivism: A response to Foley and Fumerton," *Philosophical Issues* 5, 29–50.

———— (1997), "Reflective knowledge in the best circles," *Journal of Philosophy* 94:8, 410–30.

———— (2000), "Skepticism and contextualism," *Philosophical Issues* 10, 1–18.

———— (2001), "For the love of truth?" in Abrol Fairweather and Linda Zagzebski (eds.), *Virtue epistemology: essays on epistemic virtue and responsibility* (Oxford;New York: Oxford University Press), 29–62.

———— (2003), "The place of truth in epistemology," in Michael DePaul and Linda Zagzebski (eds.), *Intellectual virtue* (Oxford: Oxford University Press).

———— (2007), *A virtue epistemology: apt belief and reflective knowledge* (Oxford;New York: Oxford University Press).

Steup, Matthias (2001), *Knowledge, truth, and duty: essays on epistemic justification, responsibility, and virtue* (Oxford;New York: Oxford University Press).

Stich, Stephen P. (1983), *From folk psychology to cognitive science: the case against belief* (Cambridge, MA: MIT Press).

———— (1990), *The fragmentation of reason: preface to a pragmatic theory of cognitive evaluation* (Cambridge, MA: MIT Press).

Stroud, Barry (1994), "Philosophical scepticism, II," *Aristotelian Society* 68, 291–307.

———— (2004), "Perceptual knowledge and epistemological satisfaction," in John Greco (ed.), *Ernest Sosa and his critics* (Malden, MA: Blackwell), 165–73.

Swain, Marshall (1978), "Epistemic defeasibility," in George Sotiros Pappas and Marshall Swain (eds.), *Essays on knowledge and justification* (Ithaca, NY: Cornell University Press).

Thagard, Paul (2000), *Coherence in thought and action* (Cambridge, MA: MIT Press).

Tye, Michael (1995), *Ten problems of consciousness: a representational theory of the phenomenal mind* (Cambridge, MA: MIT Press).

van Inwagen, Peter (2000), "Free will remains a mystery: The eighth philosophical perspectives lecture," *Philosophical Perspectives* 14, 1–19.

Walsh, W. H. (1965), "Moral authority and moral choice," *Proceedings of the Aristotelian Society* 65, 1–24.

Wells, G. L., Ferguson, T. J., and Lindsay, R. C. L. (1981), "The tractability of eyewitness confidence and its implications for triers of fact," *Journal of Applied Psychology* 66, 688–96.

Wells, G. L. and Leippe, M. R. (1981), "How do triers of fact enter the accuracy of eyewitness identification? Memory for peripheral detail can be misleading," *Journal of Applied Psychology* 66, 682–87.

Williams, Bernard Arthur Owen (1978), *Descartes: the project of pure enquiry* (Atlantic Highlands, NJ: Humanities Press).

——— (1981), *Moral luck: philosophical papers, 1973–1980* (Cambridge;New York: Cambridge University Press).

Williams, Michael (1991), *Unnatural doubts: epistemological realism and the basis of scepticism* (Oxford;Cambridge: Blackwell).

Williamson, Timothy (2000), *Knowledge and its limits* (Oxford;New York: Oxford University Press).

Woodruff, Paul (1990), "Plato's early theory of knowledge," in Stephen Everson (ed.), *Epistemology (Companions to Ancient Thought: 1)* (Cambridge: Cambridge University Press), 60–84.

Zagzebski, Linda (1994), "The inescapability of Gettier problems," *Philosophical Quarterly* 44, 65–73. Reprinted in Ernest Sosa, Jaegwon Kim, Jeremy Fantl, and Matthew McGrath (eds.), *Epistemology: an anthology* (2nd ed.; Wiley-Blackwell, 2008).

——— (1996), *Virtues of the mind: an inquiry into the nature of virtue and the ethical foundations of knowledge* (New York: Cambridge University Press).

——— (2000), "From reliabilism to virtue epistemology," in Guy Axtell (ed.), *Knowledge, belief and character: readings in virtue epistemology* (Lanham, MD: Rowman & Littlefield).

——— (2003a), "Epistemic trust," *Philosophy in the Contemporary World* 10, 113–17.

——— (2003b), "The search for the source of epistemic good," *Metaphilosophy* 34, 12–28.

——— (2004a), *Divine motivation theory* (Cambridge;New York: Cambridge University Press).

——— (2004b), "Epistemic value and the primacy of what we care about," *Philosophical Papers* 33, 353–76.

——— (2006a), "Self-trust and the diversity of religions," *Philosophic Exchange* 36.

——— (2006b), "The admirable life and the desirable life," in Timothy Chappell (ed.), *Values and virtues* (Oxford;New York: Oxford University Press).

——— (2007), "Ethical and epistemic egoism and the ideal of autonomy," *Episteme: A Journal of Social Epistemology* 4:3, 252–63.

Made in the USA
San Bernardino, CA
28 July 2016